D0060246

Praise for *Own YOUR Success*

"*Own YOUR Success* is a wonderful book with a great message. Any reader will come away with a greater passion for life and a better sense of how to grow during the journey that we're all on."

—John Schlifske
Chief Executive Officer, Northwestern Mutual

"I firmly believe that the choices we make shape our lives. Being great is also a choice, and now there is a resource available to help all of us understand the journey to greatness. *Own YOUR Success* is that resource. Read it and it will help you release your potential."

—Aeneas Williams
Future NFL Hall of Fame cornerback, 14-year NFL
veteran, and eight-time Pro Bowl player

"From the battlefield to the boardroom, I have always strived for excellence through the power of teamwork. *Own YOUR Success* will provide you with bulletproof tools to make a difference in your life and business."

—Lieutenant Bob Gassoff
United States Navy SEAL

"Ben Newman hits the ball out of the park again with *Own YOUR Success*. Against the backdrop of a captivating story, I found myself in several of the characters in the book and realized the changes that would allow me to achieve maximum, measurable success in ways that will produce greater satisfaction and happiness in life."

—Rudy Telscher
Managing Partner, Harness Dickey & Pierce;
Lead Counsel in *CBC vs. Major League Baseball*

OWN

Your

SUCCESS

OWN

Your

SUCCESS

THE **POWER** TO **CHOOSE GREATNESS** AND
MAKE EVERY DAY VICTORIOUS

BEN NEWMAN

WILEY

John Wiley & Sons, Inc.

Cover Image: Harbour Bridge and Sydney Skyline © Sara Winter/ iStockphoto
Jacket Design: C. Wallace

Published by John Wiley & Sons, Inc., Hoboken, New Jersey.
Published simultaneously in Canada.

For general information on our other products and services or for technical support,
please contact our Customer Care Department within the United States at (800)
762-2974, outside the United States at (317) 572-3993 or fax (317) 572-4002.

Wiley publishes in a variety of print and electronic formats and by print-on-demand.
Some material included with standard print versions of this book may not be
included in e-books or in print-on-demand. If this book refers to media such as a
CD or DVD that is not included in the version you purchased, you may download
this material at http://booksupport.wiley.com. For more information about Wiley
products, visit www.wiley.com.

Library of Congress Cataloging-in-Publication Data:

Newman, Ben, 1978– author.
   Own your success : the power to choose greatness and make every day
victorious / Ben Newman.
     pages cm
   Includes index.
   ISBN 978-1-118-37016-2 (cloth); ISBN 978-1-118-42080-5 (ebk);
   ISBN 978-1-118-41719-5 (ebk); ISBN 978-1-118-43185-6 (ebk)
    1. Success. I. Title
BF637.S8N447 2012
650.1—dc23

                   2012020175

Printed in the United States of America

10 9 8 7 6 5 4 3 2 1

*Dedicated to the three people who clearly help me realize
what I am fighting for every day, and for whom I am willing
to sacrifice anything: my wife, Ami, my son,
J. Isaac, and my daughter, Kennedy Rose.*

*In loving memory of
Janet Fishman Newman*

When you are inspired by some great purpose, some extraordinary project, all your thoughts break their bonds: Your mind transcends limitations, your consciousness expands in every direction, and you find yourself in a new, great, and wonderful world. Dormant forces, faculties, and talents become alive, and you discover yourself to be a greater person by far than you ever dreamed yourself to be.

—Patanjali

Contents

Acknowledgments

This book has been a special project in the making. Along the journey, many people have been tremendously supportive advocates. Special gratitude goes out to my greatest team who make all of this possible, my family: Ami, J. Isaac, and Kennedy Rose.

I would also like to acknowledge my team of Kimberly Raasch and Dusty Meehan, whose commitment to greatness every day helps me continue to fight and impact the thousands of lives we touch each year. And to Lisa Lukies, my esteemed editor, whose eagle eye on the manuscript and contribution helped to make this book the best it could be.

Additionally, the opportunity to inspire and empower others through my writing would not be possible without the stories or impact made by Dr. Jason Selk, Jon Gordon, John O'Leary, Scott Underwood, Joey Davenport, Shep Hyken, Tom Dankenbring, Todd Basler, Dr. Edward M. Johnson Jr., Bob Gassoff, Dr. Martha Skinner, John Doty, Mark Daly, Andy Kaiser, Josh Qualy, Brian Cohen, Jeff Rose, Eddie Caldwell, Josh Goodman, Heath Beam, Paul Foster, Ben Beshear, Laura Pierz, Michael Amann, Michael Kennedy Jr., and my father, Burt Newman, along with countless other family and friends who inspire me to keep fighting.

To my late mother, Janet Fishman Newman, who continues to inspire me every day to be the best I can be. You taught me life's greatest lesson, to cherish every day—*because it is not how long you live, but how you choose to live your life!*

Foreword

B en Newman has written a masterpiece. This is a book that will take you on a journey to change your life. What I love most about the book is that it speaks to the head, the heart, and the gut of the business professional in today's fast-moving world. Ben Newman has written a story through his main character, Pierce Edwards, that can relate to anybody in any facet of business today. What is so incredible about the story is that even if you are not in the business world, this book is one that will also touch your heart and change the way that you feel about your life and your legacy.

Thank you, Ben, for touching my heart with this inspirational story of getting lost on life's journey and getting yourself back on a track to greatness. I certainly believe in living life with relentless accountability to achieve greatness by using all of your capacity.

Own YOUR Success will give you the tools and the beliefs in order to make a difference in your life moving forward and to leave a dynamic legacy on the world.

—**Dr. Jason Selk**,
Best-Selling Author of *10-Minute Toughness*
and *Executive Toughness* and
Director of Sport Psychology for the 2006 and 2011
World Champion St. Louis Cardinals

Introduction

*O*wn *YOUR Success* is a powerful, modern-day fable illuminating our quest for personal and professional greatness. It's an inspiring and compassionate tale that tells the story of a 40-year-old, self-made multimillionaire, Pierce Edwards, an executive at the top of his game yet the bottom of his existence.

Though he exemplifies the "work harder and faster" mindset that he believes to be the key to success, Pierce is aware deep down that he has become disillusioned on his journey through life, and he has reluctantly begun to admit that he is adrift.

One day, his concerned wife and his best friend confront him and demand that he embark on a journey to identify his true meaning and purpose in life.

Over the next couple of weeks, Pierce meets a cast of colorful and influential characters: a CEO once trapped in the same challenges of life balance; a retired Navy SEAL; a talented high school basketball coach who himself used to play for legendary coach John Wooden; and one of the most influential doctors in the United States for the study of rare diseases.

Through this profound and life-altering journey, Pierce learns the four essential keys to great wisdom and discovers his true passion for life. He realizes with a fresh perspective that his ability to embrace change will allow him to further his success; that success itself can be measured in extraordinary ways; and that, ultimately, trusting in the greatness of others is essential to experiencing personal and professional growth.

Own YOUR Success offers the reader practical and proven exercises to transform challenges and maximize performance. The book is jam-packed with real-world advice, compelling tales, and proven strategies, and readers will uncover their true potential to create the life they were meant to fight for and enjoy personally and professionally. Providing inspiration and guidance, *Own YOUR Success* encourages individuals to embark on their own relentless pursuit of greatness.

A Note from the Author

While success comes in many guises, I firmly believe that it is bred from a single attribute: true greatness. Greatness comes in many forms; however, upon scratching the surface, one will always find elements of sacrifice.

My mentor and *Wall Street Journal* bestselling author of *The Energy Bus*, Jon Gordon, recently shared the following profound thoughts with me regarding the topic of greatness and sacrifice.

> *We can find greatness in every corner of the earth, in classrooms, locker rooms, kitchens, farms, laboratories, hospitals, nonprofit meeting rooms, factories, and in the hearts and actions of those who serve and sacrifice for a cause greater than themselves.*

- Great scientists invest their lives finding cures for cancer and other diseases.
- Great teammates sacrifice for one another.

- Great leaders selflessly serve their teams and organizations.

- Great managers give everything they have to bring out the best in others.

- Great marriages often sacrifice what each person wants for what the marriage needs.

- Great parents give of themselves to their children.

- Great social activists and entrepreneurs sacrifice money, brainpower, and resources to find new ways to improve health and economic support for people in developing countries.

- Great ministers sacrifice themselves to love and care for others.

- Great teachers sacrifice their time and energy to improve their students' lives.

- Great athletes, actors, and musicians sacrifice thousands of hours, training and developing their talents that ultimately entertain and inspire audiences.

Whether we are talking about the ultimate sacrifice our heroes make for their country, or those that people make each and every day for the good of others, the same thing always remains true: Sacrificing oneself leads to greatness, and true greatness leads to success.

So, I hope you realize that if you want to be great, you cannot simply focus on what you can accumulate for yourself. Rather, it's about how much of yourself—your time, energy, and talents—you can give to others. You may not give your

A Note from the Author

life for your country, but you *can* give your life to a cause greater than yourself. You can give selflessly to others and become *great* in their eyes.

Don't think you have to be great to serve; you merely need to be willing to serve with great desire. Wishing you great inspiration and impact on *YOUR* success journey!

Go Do Great Things!

Ben Newman

A Note from the Author

Chapter 1

Meet Pierce Edwards

Most people live life on a path that was set for them, too afraid to live on any other. But once in a while people will break down barriers and obstacles to fight to be the person they were destined to be.

—Anonymous

M eet Pierce Edwards, founder and CEO of Blackbird Technologies, a large supplier of flight technology to the United States aerospace and defense industries. Born in Charlotte, North Carolina, where he continues to make his home with his wife, Sarah, and their two children, Lila and Max, Pierce successfully turned a boyhood obsession for planes and flying into a multimillion-dollar, privately held company that employs more than 600 people—all before he reached the ripe old age of 40.

Pierce's meteoric rise to success came as no surprise to those who knew him well. Always mature beyond his years, Pierce demonstrated a relentless, unwavering drive from an extremely young age. There was never a doubt in anybody's mind that this young man would end up at the top.

A successful company in a booming industry, capped off with a beautiful family, and a stately home with all of the bells, whistles, and toys that typically accompany wealth—it seemed that Pierce really did have it all.

Or so people thought.

Recently, however, deep cracks had begun to appear in the façade of Pierce's ostensibly perfect life. He could no longer access the cool, calm demeanor he had always possessed—that he had, in fact, taken for granted—as easily. Quite simply, Pierce was losing control. Lashing out at Sarah without provocation, drinking excessively, and working later and later each evening, he was disconnecting and disengaging from human contact. He was well aware of the changes occurring within, but for the first time in his life, Pierce had no idea what to do about it.

Was this a typical case of not stopping to smell the roses, or had Pierce literally derailed somewhere along his rapid journey to the top? He couldn't be sure.

While he was navigating his black Escalade through uptown Charlotte, heading home one evening, a light mist settled over the city. Flicking the wipers to the ON position, Pierce noticed that the green clock staring out from his mahogany dashboard read 8:40 PM. Bold LED numbers crudely taunted him as he wondered when he had last made it home in time for the 6:00 news. Had he ever? He honestly could not recall.

Switching lanes, he caught his image in the rearview mirror, and was surprised to notice tufts of gray hair sprouting at the temples. When did this happen? On closer inspection, he noted that his pasty skin could use a week in the

Caribbean, or at the very least, a Sunday stroll in the park. "When did you stop caring about yourself?" Pierce asked his reflection.

Were these early physical signs of aging a fair and just ransom for his rapid rise in business and, well, *life?* Had he really matured too fast? When he was growing up, neighbors and friends had criticized his father's efforts in raising him solo. It was a father-and-son team, with one leader and one hard and fast set of rules. Naysayers abounded when Pierce was a young schoolboy, barely whispering behind cupped hands, lamenting how terrible it was what had happened to this poor young boy. A boy needed his mother and deserved the chance to be a child; and that shameful, domineering father (providing the juiciest fodder for gossips) hadn't allowed his young son the opportunity to grieve. ONWARDS AND UPWARDS was always his father's motto; there was no time to stop and think too much about anything.

Retreating from his reverie, Pierce watched as the city faded behind him. Only the Bank of America building remained in view, proudly and powerfully thrusting itself toward the heavens—the Bank of America Corporation, currently number nine on the Fortune 500 list.

Shrugging off pesky, nagging concerns that had been haunting him for months, Pierce refocused his attention on future plans for Blackbird Tech. After all, he made sacrifices all the time. So what if he had been a little stressed out? It came with the terrain, and was the only way to reach the top. Singular focus was certainly a trait Pierce had inherited from his father. One goal and one path, no matter who or what stood in the way. Sacrifice. How else would he grow the company from the largest of its kind in the United States to the largest in the world? How else would he get *himself* on that Fortune 500 list?

As Pierced turned the car into his suburban home's long, winding driveway, the gravel protested beneath his wet tires with a loud crunch. Tall poplars lined the property, cloaking the massive 30,000-square-foot home in privacy. Turning off the engine, he sat for a moment, taking it all in. He had built this home for Sarah less than five years earlier. Sacrifice, he thought smugly to himself; it's all about sacrifice.

Retrieving his sports coat and a bag of files from the back seat, Pierce made his way, as he did most nights, toward the back of the house, where he would dutifully remove his shoes before entering via the kitchen. It had become part of Pierce's routine to pass through the large, open kitchen, drop a few rocks in a glass and top it off with liquid gold, his favorite smoky, single malt, Oban, before retreating to his office—usually reemerging around 11 PM to pick at leftovers from the fridge before retiring to bed.

Tonight, however, was different.

Rounding the corner near the hothouse where Sarah tended her beloved orchids, the gentle humming of the swimming pool filter across the yard failed to conceal voices coming from inside the house. One was Sarah's and the other, which he didn't recognize immediately, was definitely male. Pierce did not recall any cars parked out front when he drove onto the property. Who was in there with Sarah? Through the window he spotted her, leaning on the granite island, her honey-blonde hair loosely cascading down her shoulders, standing in such a way that made it impossible to tell whether or not she was crying. A tall, dark-haired figure moved across the room, placing his hand on her back. He appeared to be consoling her. Pierce's mouth suddenly went dry. Josh Andrews. He tried to swallow as he picked up his pace. What the heck was Josh doing here? Had something happened to one of the kids? Why had Sarah called Josh and not Pierce? A fire burned in the pit of his gut as he burst through the kitchen door ready to confront his wife and his best friend.

Immediately hit with the thick, heavy atmosphere lingering in the kitchen, a wave of nausea washed over him. Once again, he tried to swallow, but his swollen tongue and dry mouth would not allow such freedom. He turned to Sarah, "Everything okay? Where are the kids?"

"Daddy!" Max charged across the living room, literally flying into his father's arms. Pierce scooped him up. Little Max. Thank God he was okay. Glancing across the cream-carpeted living room, he spotted Lila neatly stacking the books she'd been reading with Max on a table next to the sofa. Lila. Sweet, shy Lila. Pierce reminded himself he had less than eight years to go before his heart would be broken when she commenced dating some pimply-faced, junior-high schmuck. Max clung harder to his father—or was it Pierce doing the clinging? It was impossible to tell. Pierce desperately wanted to freeze this moment in time; his daughter young and innocent, his son loving and sweet . . . and his wife and best friend not about to tell him whatever it was they were planning. Perhaps it wasn't eight years before his heart was to break after all. Perhaps it was merely eight minutes, or seconds, away.

5

Meet Pierce Edwards

"Daddy, I missed you!" Max mumbled into Pierce's neck, digging his little hands further into Pierce's shoulders, an action filled as much with love as it was with longing.

"I missed you too, buddy." Holding Max close, the sweet scent of Johnson & Johnson baby shampoo wafted up from his freshly washed hair. Was it really Johnson's? His heart sank when he realized he did not know the answer to this. Pierce had not been a part of the kids' bath time ritual for several years now. Sarah could be using engine oil on their hair and he'd be none the wiser.

"Daddy, you're home! We waited up to say goodnight!" Lila exclaimed as she joined her brother, curling her limbs around Pierce's legs and torso. An old, wise tree at the mercy of a rampant, youthful vine, Pierce waited patiently while the kids, wiggling in his arms, excitedly relayed the events of their day.

Kissing the tops of the children's heads, he bid them good night, waited as they kissed Sarah and "Uncle Josh" good night, and watched them run upstairs, hand in hand, their matching Paul Frank pajamas swaying in unison. Lila was a good kid, responsible, a really good big sister to Max. Six years old, wow, he had to remember that. Time was slipping by. And how old was Max now? Four? Jeez.

Dreading the challenging conversation that was sure to follow, Pierce stalled, "Shouldn't one of us be reading them a bedtime story?"

Sarah sighed. "Honey, Lila read to Max already. They're good for tonight. I promise." Maintaining eye contact, she smiled, one of her warm, disarming smiles.

For a moment Pierce thought he misread the entire scenario and the knot in his gut released a little as his tongue peeled itself away from the roof of his mouth. That was before Sarah added, "We need to talk."

Eyeing Josh and Sarah suspiciously, Pierce reached for a rocks glass sitting on a shelf in the cabinet above the sink. "Wait," Sarah stopped him, "I opened a nice bottle of cabernet, it's decanting in the dining room. I thought we might enjoy it together, the three of us."

"Well la-de-dah, Lady Sarah," Pierce wanted to say, "Look at you, going out in style! Probably spent a king's ransom on a posh cabernet—decanting as we speak, no less—to ceremoniously enjoy with your *boyfriend* while your plans to divorce are announced." Instead, Pierce coolly placed the glass back on the middle shelf and quietly made his way to the dining room while he raged internally. How did he let this happen? For weeks, months even, he had felt his life slowly unraveling; but *this*, he did not foresee.

Taking a seat at the head of the dining table, Sarah watched as Josh poured the heavy, red wine into the three glasses she had laid out earlier. Pierce, intent on holding on to some dignity, thanked Josh for his wine as he took residence in the seat perpendicular to Sarah's, immediately regretting his choice when Josh sat directly opposite him. "Don't crack," he told himself. "Save face, buddy."

Swirling the deep burgundy liquid in the glass, Pierce joked, "I'd raise a toast. But, I've no idea what we should be drinking to."

Sarah reached across the table, gently placing her hand over his. He resisted the urge to pull away from her.

"Honey, relax. We didn't mean to ambush you, it's just . . . it's just kind of difficult to get you to commit to anything

7

Meet Pierce Edwards

other than work lately. Short of making an appointment with your secretary, I saw no other way for us to all get together."

"Okay. Well, here I am." Pierce loathed the fact he could not control the emotion in his voice.

"Buddy, Sarah and I ran to each other last week at the grocery store. We're concerned about you. That's all."

Pierce could not stop the laughter bubbling up in him. "Concerned? What's to be concerned about?"

"Pierce, did you see my car out front when you came in?" Josh held up his hand, stopping Pierce from answering, "No, you didn't, because I *walked* here. I live four blocks away. Four. And I haven't seen you in over five months."

Sighing, Pierce slouched back in his seat, relieved and slightly amused by his gross misinterpretation of the scene. "What are you talking about? We had breakfast a few weeks ago."

"Actually, I had breakfast with a stranger who barely ate, barely talked, and typed on his BlackBerry the entire time . . . in *May*. We're in October, bud."

Pierce flushed as a bubble of resentment rose within him; he did not enjoy being put on the spot.

"When I ran into Sarah," Josh continued, "she burst into tears when I asked about you." Stung, Pierce looked to Sarah, who quietly stared at her wine glass.

"Honey?"

Sarah continued staring as if the words she needed would magically appear in the glass at any given moment.

The three friends sat in silence. Only the faint ticking of a clock could be heard off in the distance. Pierce struggled to recall even owning an analog clock. He certainly had no idea in which room it was housed. Each tick felt like an eternity and he longed to find the source of the noise and smash it into a million pieces. But he was glued to his seat, unable to move, as he waited for his wife to speak.

Sarah nervously curled her lower lip inward and gently bit down on it. "Please, please don't cry," Pierce willed her. She looked down at her hands, nervously fidgeting with her wedding band. Spinning the diamond pavé ring around her long and slender ring finger with the thumb and index finger of her right hand, she looked up at Pierce and found the courage to speak. "Honey, something has to change. You're no longer the man I married." She paused, struggling to control her emotions. "Believe me—I am *beyond* appreciative for the lifestyle you have provided for our family. Building your company required incredible commitment and a lot of hard work and I certainly understand the priority it takes in your life . . . *our* lives. But, I need you present. So do the kids. Without you, this house, the cars, the lifestyle . . . well, it really doesn't mean anything at all."

Pierce remained silent. He recognized the importance of what Sarah was trying to say; yet he had no idea how to respond, or how he could fix it.

"When Josh asked about you, my heart broke. Josh has been your best friend since grade school . . . and he'd not seen or heard from you in months. I could not wrap my head, or my heart, around understanding what changed in you. When did you stop caring about the people who should matter most? It's not who you used to be."

Josh spoke next. "Financial and business success is just a small slice on the pie-chart, buddy. You told me that, years

9

ago, just after graduation. Family, health, friends, *a life*, are of equal importance. Attaining—and maintaining—balance; that's the mark of a truly successful individual."

Pierce cringed, embarrassed by the recollection of his pompous, immature, college-boy lectures. As if reading his thoughts, Josh said, "Yeah, you were young and inexperienced and probably didn't have a clue what you were talking about back then. But there was a lot of truth to that piece of unsolicited wisdom you so generously handed out." Josh smiled at his friend. "You nailed it—the mark of a successful individual."

"It's also the mark of a healthy one," Sarah added. "Pierce, we miss you. We miss your laugh, your smile, and your presence. Our biggest fear is not losing you to your work; it's losing you to a heart attack or something. All you *do* is work. You come home late, holing yourself up in your office. You rarely eat, but you do *drink*. When was the last time you saw the inside of a gym . . . or even your sneakers?"

"Sarah's right . . . and I do miss my jogging partner."

Pierce rested his head in his hands. What a chump he'd been. Here he was thinking Sarah was running off with Josh—which she probably *should!*—and there she was, giving him the chance to make things right. Josh too. He thought back to his last meeting with Josh. Had it really been five months ago? He'd treated his time with his best friend as obligatory at best, a mandatory stop on his way to more important things. Josh was right; he really had spent most his time that morning on his BlackBerry. What a jerk.

Deeply sighing, Pierce reached for his wine, raising it in the air as he spoke, "Here's to interventions. No longer

reserved for alcoholics and drug abusers, but class-A jerks!"
Laughter filled the room as their glasses clinked, shattering a
heavy tension the air had been nursing from the moment
Pierce walked in the door.

"I promise to be more attentive. Work's really hectic right
now, but I promise you . . . *both* of you. I'll figure out a way
to find more time." He looked toward Josh. "To run and hang
out, catch a game or two. Like old times." And then to Sarah,
"To spend more time with you and the kids."

Josh and Sarah exchanged looks as Pierce pressed on.
"Honey, in a few months, during holiday season, we'll take
the kids on vacation. A cruise, Disneyland, anywhere you
want to go."

"Pierce," Sarah said firmly, "you're missing the point."
Swallowing hard, turning to Josh for reassurance, she added,
"We don't need a vacation. You do."

Pierce was stunned. What did she mean by *that*?

"Pierce, this is not a quick-fix problem. You've worked
yourself into the ground and a very big part of you got lost on
the way. It's been manifesting for months . . . years even.
You've changed and I don't like who you are right now. Take
some time, do some soul searching. Please, for the sake of
our family, get back in touch with who you are and what you
really want." She paused for effect. "Pierce, you need to do
this if our marriage is to survive."

The ticking clock got louder. Or was it Pierce's own heart
thumping, that deafening sound rising up in his ears? "Are
you asking me to move out?"

"Heavens, no! But you do need to get away for a bit, a
retreat of sorts." Sarah reached for a file and opened it before

sliding it across the table in front of Pierce. Looking down, he saw an e-ticket for an American Airlines flight to Colorado and a copy of an e-mail confirmation for accommodations. "I—I took the liberty of booking a cabin in the Colorado mountains. I know how much you enjoyed being there all those years ago. This is the best gift you could give yourself. Stop, take stock in your life—and find your passion and your truth again." She walked over to where Pierce sat, draped her arms around his neck, and kissed him tenderly on top of his head. "You need to do this now, Pierce, before it's too late."

That gnawing, nagging feeling of emptiness Pierce had been fighting for months arose. Though he loathed to admit it, Sarah was right. He now realized that this attitude wasn't just affecting him; it was taking a toll on his family and friends as well. He knew he had to agree.

"Okay, honey, I think you're onto something here. I'll look into this retreat idea and we'll figure out some time for me to go, probably between the holidays and the New Year when things quiet down a bit."

Tears welled up in Sarah's eyes. "Pierce, you don't understand. I've already booked the trip. You leave tomorrow."

Pierce pushed his seat back from the table, almost knocking Sarah to the ground, wildly pacing the room, arms flailing. "The Colorado mountains? *Tomorrow?* Are you insane? I can't just go off meditating on a snow-filled mountaintop in the middle of *October*—the beginning of the fourth, and final, quarter! Why not send me to Tibet, or the bloody moon? One way!"

"Pier—"

"No!" He cut her off. *"No."* Pausing, reining in his emotions, a long moment passed before he turned back to Sarah. "I appreciate what you are saying. Every word. More than you know. Yes, changes have been occurring; I've noticed them too . . . the way I feel . . . talk . . . think . . . do business. But honey, I can't just up and leave. The timing needs to be right."

"Sometimes the right time never comes; you just have to jump in," Josh piped up.

"Don't tell me—Pierce Edwards, circa 1993."

Josh grinned. "Yup."

"Schmuck," Pierce murmured, more to himself than Josh.

Placing his hands on Sarah's shoulders, he looked her directly in the eyes. "I promise to go over my schedule this week and find the right time to get away . . . but please, call the retreat in the morning and cancel the reservation." Kissing her tenderly on the forehead, he added, "I'll see you in bed."

"Josh, it's really good to see you. I'm glad you came around tonight." He hugged Josh before heading out the door.

"Anderson was all set to take over Blackbird for a short time." It was Sarah who spoke, stopping Pierce in his tracks.

"Anderson?"

"Yes. Phillips. Your company VP."

Pierce's head spun wildly. He did not trust anyone else at the helm of Blackbird. Not even his VP—*not anyone.* The very thought of it gave him a splitting headache. "Well, then you should probably call him in the morning too." Turning on his heel, he made his way upstairs, leaving a disheartened Josh and Sarah in his wake.

13

Meet Pierce Edwards

Pierce sneaked along the broad hallway upstairs to check on the kids before retiring to his office. Max's room was nearest. His tiny body sprawled across the shiny, red sports car bed, and toys were strewn all over the room. Pierce took them all in—robots, planes, balls, cars, trains, trucks, and bikes. When does a kid have time to play with all of those things, he wondered. A sliver of light shone through the curtains. Pierce padded lightly across the floor, dodging toys along the way, to close them. Looking out across the yard from the window in Max's room, the sight of the swimming pool sparkling in the moonlight gave him pause. A damn swimming pool! Did he really believe the toys, the pool, the private school tuition, buying every damn thing the kids wanted made up for his absence? Did any of this really substitute for a present and engaged parent? Pulling the covers over Max's tiny body, all the way to his dimpled chin, Pierce leaned down to kiss him, very gently, taking great care not to wake him.

Moments later, just down the hall, he peered into Lila's room, an explosion of every possible shade of pink. Six! He still could not believe it. Leaning against the solid doorframe, he fingered the pink satin ballet slippers hanging from its handle. Shame washed over him.

"You broke her heart, you know." Sarah's voice, a cold hushed whisper, startled him. Pierce bristled with anger as the guilt he harbored deep within put him on the defensive.

"I was in meetings, Sarah. You know that." The edge to his voice sounded colder when lowered to a whisper.

"A meeting you could have easily delegated to one of your engineers, Pierce." She glared fiercely at her husband, delicate nostrils flaring with rage. "*Firsts* are just that, Pierce. They only ever happen once. No repeats, no undoing, or redoing. I only hope you understand all you are missing before it is too late." Turning, she made her way downstairs, a whirlwind of pent-up frustration and disappointment whipping the air around her.

Watching Sarah storm back downstairs, he knew she was right. He could attend every ballet recital, every dress rehearsal, even each and every class Lila took, but his first-born and only daughter would have but one first ballet recital, and he had missed it. Looking in on his sleeping daughter, he choked down the lump rising in this throat. He had broken her heart.

Listening to her soft, rhythmic breathing, he wondered what she dreamt about. Trying to conjure dreams of a six-year-old only triggered memories of the nightmare that was his sixth birthday. The candles, the big, colorful cake . . . the two empty seats at the dining table where his brother and mother usually sat. Pierce closed his eyes as the familiar, painful sting of this memory ripped through him. It had been way too soon. Not quite a month. It was his father who had insisted upon the party, but his supreme effort to create a sense of normality only served to highlight their absence. The two empty seats, staring back at him in the flickering candlelight, had winded young Pierce.

"Make a wish, make a wish," his father and aunt sang out cheerfully. Even as a young, heartbroken six-year-old, Pierce was wise enough to know the one thing he longed for could never happen, no matter how hard he wished: his mother and brother to take a different route that sunny Saturday afternoon after the soccer game. There would be no detour for an ice

15

Meet Pierce Edwards

ream cone, rewarding Billy for his goal. No crossing the old railroad tracks at 1:34 PM. No faulty signal. No oncoming train. Gasping, Pierce had struggled to blow the candles out. Fighting back tears, trying to force the air out, when all it wanted to do was rush back in, in heaving gulps. Aunt Joanna leaned in beside him, blowing out the six candles on his behalf. "Good boy," she whispered, gently rubbing his back.

Aunt Joanna. Pierce smiled at her memory. What a gift she had been, stepping in to pick up the pieces his father dropped along the way. She was wise enough to know that she could never fill the void in his young heart. And she was wise enough to allow Pierce's father to believe he was doing it all on his own, and doing a grand job. Pierce knew his father did the very best he could, and that he was consumed by his own grief the entire time. Pierce never had the heart to dissect or criticize any aspect of his upbringing, but still he was grateful for Joanna. Sweet Joanna, who allowed him to cry and pretended not to see, who picked him up from school early to have the too-big uniforms altered and then realtered when a growth spurt hit—all without his father knowing.

He had not seen Aunt Joanna in years. Granted, she now lived in San Francisco—which Pierce knew was a petty, lame excuse for allowing another important person to drift out of his life. Or was Pierce the one doing the drifting?

Turning away from Lila's room, he noticed the light fanning out from beneath the master bedroom door, long, golden tentacles stretching down the hallway. Sarah must already be in there, he figured. Uncertain of how long he had been daydreaming in the kids' rooms, Pierce made a beeline for the office.

16

Own YOUR Success

Sitting at his desk, he quickly typed an e-mail to Anderson Phillips. Snapping his laptop closed, he joined Sarah in the bedroom. She looked beautiful, sitting up in bed, reading a paperback. Smiling sheepishly, he strode across the room toward the his-and-hers walk-in closets. His was on the left, Sarah's to the right. The standard joke around the house was that women—and Sarah especially—were always right. Tonight had been no exception.

As he placed the carry-on on the chair, Sarah slowly lowered the book onto her lap. "You're going?" She whispered, her voice a raspy blend of disbelief and joy.

"I'm going." Pierce smiled. "What time's the Denver flight?"

"7:30 AM."

"AM? Wow. You really *do* want to get rid of me. When's the return booked?"

Sarah made her way over to where Pierce stood and began to help him pack. "Honey, I didn't book a return, it's up to you. You'll know when you're ready to come home."

"Shouldn't be more than a few days," he promised.

Zipping up the black carry-on, Sarah stopped him by placing her hand over his. "Take all the time you need. We'll all be here when you're ready to come home." Smiling, she added, "If you do it right the first time, you'll only have to do it once."

"Is that another Pierce-ism?"

"I think so."

"You married a pretty corny guy, didn't you?" Laughing, they climbed into bed together for the last time before Pierce embarked on his journey.

Chapter 2

The Journey Begins

One day your life will flash before your eyes. Make sure it
is worth watching.

—**Unknown**

Pierce generously tipped his cab driver upon arriving at
Charlotte Douglas International Airport, grateful for the
ride without conversation. But the silence in the cab certainly
did not make up for the lack of silence in Pierce's head.
A whirlpool of activity spun wildly—a boisterous cacophony
he'd been unable to switch off since agreeing to Sarah's plan.

Doubts, concerns, and fears lingered. What was he
thinking, leaving Anderson at the helm? Did his employees
respect Anderson enough to follow his lead? Was this really
worth it—the time and the risk he was taking? What if he let
Sarah and the kids down anyway? What would really change?
Even if he did "find his truth" as Sarah had put it—well, what
then? Could he—would he—change his daily routine and
professional goals to accommodate what he learned? He knew
that he absolutely needed to find a way to spend more time
with the family; there was no doubt he had lost his way there.

So why the hell was he getting on a plane alone, to fly more than 1,500 miles *away* from them?

Pierce squeezed his eyes shut, pounding his forehead with a closed fist. He stopped, however, when he heard Sarah's voice powerfully silencing the buzzing swarm of thoughts: "Pierce, you need to do this if our marriage is to survive."

Slamming the car's trunk closed, he extended the handle on his carry-on, wheeling it behind him as he made his way to the American Airlines kiosk to print his boarding pass. The compact Victorinox luggage allowed him the advantage of heading directly to security, bypassing the long line of people snaking around the ticket counter.

A fairly frequent traveler, Pierce whizzed through the first class lane at the security check point, dropping his shoes, watch, BlackBerry, and belt in the white plastic tub before placing it on the conveyer belt next to his bag. He was in and out of there in less than 10 minutes. Stopping at a Hudson News stand to pick up copies of *USA Today* and *Wall Street Journal*, he could not help but notice row upon row of glossy business magazines, half of which bore titles he'd never heard of. Like the one directly in front of him: *Success!* Scoffing, he rolled his eyes at the idiocy of such a title. Oh, please, he thought, I already *am* successful. Eyeing the taglines on the cover of *Success Leveraging for Profit; Staying on Top without Burning Out; Meet the Man Behind BBA Health: Celebrating Four-Plus Years at Forbes #12*—his cockiness gave way to curiosity, and he tucked the magazine on top of the two newspapers and grabbed a bottle of water and packet of gum.

Sitting there, to the left of the register—beside bright colorful displays of candy, and clearly out of place—were stacks of notebooks of varying size and color. Pierce laughed as what appeared to be a new-age twist of universal intervention—which he absolutely did not believe in—manifested. Wherever his inward journey was heading, he knew journaling would play a key role in accessing the root of his desires, goals, and, priorities. He reasoned that it would put him back in touch with his inner voice, silenced long ago by the alluring song of profits and gains. He selected a 300-page, spiral-bound book with a thick, sturdy black cover, along with two black ink gel roller-balls. He thought for a minute, switched the notebook for one with 500 pages, and paid the cashier.

Noticing that the boarding process had commenced at the gate, Pierce quickened his pace to a light jog. Even in first class, overhead bin space was valuable, and Pierce did not want to lose out and be forced to check his luggage. Slow-moving security lines and long waits at the luggage carousel were his biggest sources of irritation while traveling. While his expertise might be in flight technology, he was certain that opportunities abound to create better systems on the ground. Squeezing his luggage into the last, tiny space available—since when did a duffle holding what looks like a 300-pound body qualify as a carry-on?—Pierce chastised his entrepreneurial mental overdrive. This trip's purpose, after all, was about lessening his load, not creating more work.

The gentleman seated next to him was already snoring, and Pierce, once again, was grateful for the gift of peace and quiet. Time to think. Thoughts of Anderson and Blackbird

Tech came raging through his mind uncontrollably, like a burst storm drain rushing a crowded city street. "Anderson Phillips? Oh God! What am I doing? I've not even briefed him. And who knows what Sarah told him—am I insane?" He was muttering to himself.

"Excuse me?" Jolted back to reality, Pierce looked up to discover the bright smile of a stewardess beaming back at him. "Great," he thought, "raving mad."

"I'll take a coffee, please. Cream, no sugar." He smiled back, hoping she had in fact come by to offer refreshments.

Sipping on the warm, stale brew (also high up on his commercial aviation travel flaw list), Pierce scrolled through his BlackBerry for upcoming appointments; he would be calling Anderson as soon as he landed in Denver. Sarah had booked a private cabin in Woodland Park, a 90-minute drive from the airport—which gave Pierce ample time to relay his instructions to his second-in-command. He'd sugar-coat it a little, but essentially he needed to tell Anderson not to do, say, change, order, or discuss *anything* without his input. He'd then call his secretary, Nora, and have her push any important meetings back until his return. Easy enough.

Pierce never had been very good at delegating respon-sibility to others. It was a weakness he was made aware of in business school, and one that he most likely inherited, or learned, from his father. This brought a whole new fear to light: Was he becoming his father? Isn't this what psycholo-gists claimed eventually happened to all of us? Pushing thoughts of Anderson and his father aside, Pierce reached for his notebook, attempting to redirect his focus to himself.

Pierce divided the first page of his new notebook into two equal columns. In the first, top line and center, he wrote *Personal Achievements*, and in the second, *Professional Achievements*. Underlining each heading with black lines, he proceeded to list his items for each column.

Personal Achievements	Professional Achievements
Dean's list UNC	Columbia MBA Program
Boston Marathon (qualify and complete)	Negotiating BBT start-up funds in college
Kids/Sarah/House	Defense (govt.) contract for BBT

Memories percolated within, spilling out of the pen and onto the page. The more he wrote, the more he remembered, including things and people he had not thought about in years. He wrote steadily, filling several pages in his neat, cursive hand.

A satisfied smile stretched across his face as he sat back and reviewed his lists. Swelling with pride, he felt like a contestant on that old show he and his father used to watch reruns of. The show whose host Joanna claimed was related to them, without ever providing solid evidence to back her claim. What was his name? Something . . . Edwards? Richard? Ron? He couldn't be sure. Closing his eyes, Pierce could hear Mr. Edwards's (whatever his name was) firm, timbre voice: "Pierce Edwards, *This* is your life."

Basking in his accomplishments, Pierce was shocked when the jet's wheels lowered in preparation for landing.

Where had the time gone? He hadn't even glanced at his newspapers.

He looked beyond his snoring neighbor to the snow-kissed mountains in the distance. A light flurry dusted the runway; an early, unpredictable snow was not uncommon in these parts. Still, the pilot—a veteran of unpredictable weather—landed with ease.

Wheeling his luggage toward the Hertz counter, Pierce tried Anderson on his cell phone. No answer. He tried him at the office; again, no answer. His nostrils flared as he struggled to contain his anger. Hitting the speed dial he left a message for Nora, commanding her to hunt Anderson down and have him call back immediately. Where the heck was he? And where the hell was Nora? Checking his watch, still set to east coast time, he knew it was too early for lunch. Where were they? Regret and doubt clouded his mind once again.

"This snow going to back off?" Pierce sidled up to the rental car counter, passing his credit card to the clerk so she could look up the reservation.

"Don't look like it. Where you heading, sir?" Not looking up from her computer screen, clicking madly at the keys, she tapped Pierce's name into the system.

"Woodland Park area."

"You hitting the road now?"

"As soon as you process my rental. That's the plan, unless you tell me otherwise."

Checking her watch, she made the calculation, "You should be okay. But head straight there, all right? Big storm coming our way later."

"Really? When?"

"Four, five o'clock. Hope you don't need to get back in a hurry. The city's real good at clearing roads after a storm, but it takes a little longer to get things done up in the mountains."

Pierce swallowed hard. He did *not* want to be trapped in the wilderness for weeks on end. "Don't worry," the clerk assured him upon noticing his reaction. "It's never more than a day or two." She click-clacked away at the keyboard while Pierce, once again, questioned his sanity.

"Aha. Here you are . . . ohhh." A worried expression painted the woman's face, the faint lines across her forehead morphed into deep valleys as she squinted at the screen, rapidly punching more keys.

"Okay, Pierce?" she looked up at him, smiling. "Seems you booked a Mustang convertible for your journey into the mountains. A fun choice and I hate to rain on your parade, but it's no match for the weather we've got coming. I have one remaining all-wheel-drive vehicle, a Suzuki SX4. Kind of small and it's a stick shift. But it *will* be much safer. What do you think?"

"Absolutely fine. Does it have GPS?"

"Sorry, we're all out. I can print Mapquest directions if you like."

"No, it's okay; I'll pull it up on my BlackBerry." Checking the brass tag pinned to her blouse, he added, "Thanks, Melissa."

Melissa was right; the Suzuki was minute compared to his Escalade. Moving the driver's seat back as far as it would go, Pierce climbed in. Squeezing behind the wheel, he felt as though he were attempting to ride a tiny, teacup poodle like a horse. His knees angled up toward his ears as he tested the

25

The Journey Begins

clutch with his left foot. Being crammed in a small space wasn't the only thing that felt foreign; he'd not driven a stick in years. At least most of the driving would be a straight stretch, and just like his mind, he could leave it in overdrive.

Heading along East 470 toward highway 25, Pierce felt a knot forming in the pit of his stomach that he chalked up to nerves. In addition to his soul-searching mission, he had a new reason to feel anxious: arriving at his destination before the storm hit. He scanned the radio, found an easy-listening station, and cranked up the volume in an attempt to drown out his thoughts and enjoy the ride. The light snow continued for most of the journey, making an already idyllic scene prettier. Any sign of an oncoming storm remained to be seen and the benign snowfall, if anything, appeared to be slowing. Pierce finally began to relax and enjoy the bucolic surroundings.

Cruising along highway 25, the knot in his gut returned, pulsing and fuming, as he remembered anxiety number three: Anderson.

He dialed Anderson's number once again, only to receive his voice mail. Pounding the steering wheel, Pierce let loose. "Damn you, Anderson!" He tossed the phone aside angrily. It bounced off the passenger seat and onto the floor, Pierce's hot frustration a stark contrast to the cool, soft flurries falling from the sky.

Pierce's inability to reach Anderson only fueled his foul mood with ruminating, negative thoughts, and led to a deeper sense of frustration. He decided to get off at the next exit ramp, turn around, and take the next flight home. His most desperate hope now was catching a flight before they were all grounded. The idea of vying for space at an overcrowded airport hotel hardly appealed to him.

As he turned off a remote exit ramp outside of Colorado Springs, Pierce's heart leapt to his throat when the phone rang. Anderson! Finally. An attempt to blindly fumble for the phone was fruitless. Taking his eyes off the road for a split second, Pierce ducked under the dash to retrieve it, still crying out to be answered, but it cut off the minute he wrapped his hands around the device. He threw it on the seat in a fit of rage and turned back to the wheel, just in time to see a large buck deer standing defiantly in the middle of the road.

But not in time to stop.

■ ■ ■

Pierce's head pounded as he slowly opened his eyes. He blinked, taking in his surroundings, and desperately tried to piece together where he was—and what had happened. Dusk had fallen, and his hand—caked in dried blood— trembled as he reached for the door handle. He felt dazed as he stumbled out of the crumpled mess of metal that his rental car had become. He could make out a log fence in the distance, destroyed and flattened—evidently by him. Beyond the fence he could see the embankment, the exit ramp a long, steep climb above it. He held his head in a vain attempt to stop the pulsing, thumping pain, and struggled to recall what had clearly been a terrible accident.

Soft flurries had now given way to a harsh and heavy snow. Furious snowflakes like sharp little ice picks stabbed viciously at his face. Pierce tried to walk, but an intense, paralyzing pain jolted through him, from his knee to his brain, immobilizing him. He tried again, hopping on his good leg, dragging the lame one. Each bounce amplified the pounding in his head while pain ricocheted throughout his body in all directions. Stumbling to the ground, his face pressed hard against the cruel, numbing cold, Pierce began to crawl in a fit of desperation, helplessly surrendering as the pure white snow faded to black.

Chapter 3

Attaining Belief in Yourself

The First Encounter

Above all, be true to yourself, and if you cannot put your heart in it, take yourself out of it.

—Hardy D. Jackson

The faint scent of sandalwood tickled Pierce's nose. Feeling warm and snug amongst the soft, plump pillows and blankets supporting him made him acutely aware of the freezing icepack strapped to his head. Reaching up, he gently touched the pack, gingerly patting it, a blind man exploring his surroundings.

"Here, let me get that." The alien tone startled Pierce; he'd expected to hear Sarah's voice, not a man's. Warm air rushed in, kissing his cool forehead as the stranger gently peeled the ice pack away. "You had quite an accident, my friend."

"Who are you?" Pierce rasped, trying to sit up, the pain in his head vengefully returning the instant he moved. "Ouch . . . Argggh." He froze, holding his head in his hands, willing the pain to stop.

29

"It's okay, take your time . . . slowly now . . . I'm Jon." The stranger smiled warmly and offered, "Would you like some water?" Pierce nodded, regretting it immediately as his head throbbed in protest. Jon helped Pierce to sit up, plumping pillows and propping them behind him. Even as he carefully sat very, very still, Pierce felt like a Mexican marching troupe was stomping wildly inside his head.

He took in the unfamiliar surroundings as he suspiciously watched Jon cross the spartan room and fill a glass with water from a carafe. An open fire cracked and popped, sending a pleasant, radiant heat across the room—and a couple of large pillar candles provided the room's only light. Aside from the large comfortable sofa upon which he rested, there wasn't a lot of furniture or personal items around. From where he sat, this contemporary, minimalist home—with its floor-to-ceiling glass and heavy wooden beams—looked big and expensive. Yet this simple man—dressed in maroon cotton drawstring pants and matching shirt, complete with Chinese collar— seemed an unlikely tenant. As Jon walked toward him, Pierce noticed the mala beads snaked around his left wrist. Was he a monk, he wondered?

Yet the oddest thing about Jon was that, somehow, he looked vaguely familiar to Pierce.

As he handed Pierce two aspirin along with his water, Jon took a seat, lotus style, on a small floor cushion. He sat quietly, watching Pierce.

Gulping the aspirin down, Pierce wondered why this freakish man was staring at him. It made him uncomfortable, and paranoia set in as he wondered if perhaps he had just swallowed something that wasn't aspirin. He had no idea what Jon wanted, and had little desire to hang around and find out. Placing the empty water glass on a small side table, Pierce pushed the blankets aside and swung his legs around to sit on the sofa's edge. Crippling pain surged to his core as his left leg, held stick-straight in a splint, banged against the solid coffee table.

Jon remained in his perfect lotus, a knowing smile on his face.

"What's so amusing, psycho?" Pierce angrily thought to himself.

"Your knee is badly twisted and sprained," Jon finally said after several moments.

Pierce glared hotly at him, not saying a word. He didn't have to; his wrath was obvious to both men.

Still Jon did not budge; his calm demeanor only caused Pierce's irritation to grow.

"Well, do you mind telling me where I am?" Pierce snapped.

"Not at all," Jon beamed. Warmth shone from his eyes, which had an adverse effect on Pierce. He distrusted this unflappable individual more and more with each passing moment.

"You are on my private retreat, just outside of Colorado Springs." Gesturing beyond the enormous panes of glass, Jon added, "And, as you can see, Mother Nature is treating us to a lovely blizzard."

Pierce narrowed his eyes. Jon's cheerful attitude rubbed him the wrong way. "And how did I get here?"

"Chance. Luck." Jon chuckled softly. "This house sits on 200 acres of wilderness. You're incredibly fortunate that I like

31

Attaining Belief in Yourself

to take my snowmobile out for a spin when we get heavy snow."

A monk on a snowmobile. Now he'd heard everything.

"You crashed through the furthest perimeter of my property. It appears you rolled down the embankment near an exit ramp off highway 25. It's a miracle you survived the crash, let alone lying out there in the snow. The engine felt cold to the touch. I can only guess you'd been there several hours."

An image of a buck standing stock still, its massive antlers like giant crossbows flashed through Pierce's mind—a target he did not want to hit. The memory came charging toward him now: He had swerved sharply, but still had no chance to brake or decelerate as the small rental car took flight, careening over the embankment. Pierce strained to remember more, but failed.

"You should get some rest. I'll help you to the guest room. I think you'll sleep better in there."

"Fine," Pierce snapped, cringing at his tone. After all, this man had saved his life. Without him, he'd still be lying face down in the snow, most likely buried by this blizzard.

"Are you hungry? I can bring you some soup," Jon offered as he helped Pierce up, taking most of the injured man's weight on his lean, muscular body.

"No, thank you." Pierce worked hard to remove the edge from his voice.

Surprised by his strength, Pierce now understood how Jon had managed to get his heavy, unconscious body onto a snowmobile and into the house. He was practically carrying him on his back, effortlessly making his way across the massive living space.

32

Jon carefully lowered Pierce onto what felt like a bed; he couldn't know for sure, since the room was pitch dark. Retrieving a flashlight from his pocket, Jon moved about the room, expertly lighting candles. Placing the flashlight next to Pierce, he said, "You might need this. Power's been down all day. Sure I can't bring you some soup?"

"I'm fine," Pierce said softly, humbled by this stranger's kindness.

"Very well. I'll check in later, in case you change your mind."

"My name's Pierce," he offered meekly as Jon left the room.

"I know." Jon smiled back at Pierce, gently closing the door behind him. Pierce listened as Jon's bare feet padded along the floorboards, back toward the living area. How did he know his name?

The room he was in felt more like a library than a guest room. Not unlike the living room, its decor was tasteful and elegant; yet hundreds of books lined a floor-to-ceiling bookshelf. Finally, Pierce thought, a sign of life, or at the very least, some personality. To the left of the bookshelves an entire wall of glass took the place of a window, but it was too dark to see what lay beyond it. In front of that wall stood some kind of altar. A large gold Buddha, glittering in the candlelight, peered back at Pierce. Flanked by thick rods of burning incense, delicate curls of smoke drifted heavenwards in a silent dance. Sandalwood.

Noticing his luggage tucked neatly in the corner along with a clear plastic trash bag holding his Tod's loafers, cashmere sports coat, jeans, and sweater, Pierce was suddenly cognizant

Attaining Belief in Yourself

of the gray sweatpants and T-shirt he was now wearing. Pulling on the shirt to read its logo without moving his head, he was surprised to see the Harvard logo smiling back at him. "A monk who went to Harvard and rides snowmobiles," Pierce scoffed to himself in disbelief. It reminded him vaguely of a book title. Something he had read long ago, before an inflated ego elevated him to higher plains, where other people's inspiring stories seemed a waste of precious time.

Standing between his belongings and a comfortable-looking leather armchair were his wallet, BlackBerry, the newspapers and magazines he had purchased in Charlotte, and his new journal. Pierce almost leapt out of bed when his eyes fixed on the BlackBerry. He needed to call Sarah! Most importantly, that small electronic device, sitting impartially on the table, held within in it the powerful possibility of getting him out of this strange place. Hope sat less than 10 feet away from him, staring him in the face. The only problem was figuring out how to retrieve it with his injured leg. He decided once again to crawl, dragging his splinted leg behind him like an injured dog, and carefully slid to the edge of the bed. *Swoosh.* His head objected, spinning fiercely. Catching his breath for a moment, he spotted his salvation: Passively leaning against the post at the end of the bed stood a gnarly, twisted wooden staff. A walking stick! A walking stick *and* his BlackBerry! Agnostic (at best), Pierce still could not resist smiling at the golden Buddha. "Thank you," he whispered to the smoky, scented air.

Inching his way across the room, Pierce eased himself into the buttery-soft leather chair. He checked his wallet and discovered everything intact, and felt shame wash over him almost immediately. Only his driver's license had been removed, sitting on top of his wallet instead of inside the little slot next to his Amex, Visa, and MasterCard. Chastened, he reached for and powered up the BlackBerry. Despite the cracked screen, his heart filled with joy as it lit up. Yes! However, his joy swiftly rearranged itself into disappointment when he learned he had no signal. Dropping his head in his hands, drained of all hope, he reluctantly surrendered to the fact that he was stuck in the middle of nowhere, helpless and dependent on a random stranger who appeared to be channeling Gandhi.

Accepting defeat, he hobbled toward the wall of books and perused Jon's collection. Not one novel or novella graced the shelves. No business journals. No crime or romance paperback trash. Nothing. Not even nonfiction titles addressing fancied hobbies such as photography or antique car collecting. Each book fell into one of the following categories: self-help, spiritual mumbo-jumbo, Eastern philosophy, or art. Fishing from the bottom of the barrel, Pierce selected the least intimidating book he could find: *100 Poems to Read Before You Die*. Given his recent brush with death, he enjoyed the irony of this selection.

Propped up in bed, reading by flashlight invited memories of his teenage years, when he would study flight manuals well into the night, hidden under the covers from a father who did not share his dream to become a pilot. He could see his father shooting down that dream now, dramatically raising one finger in the air to emphasize each point . . . No money in that . . . *One* . . . Little room for growth . . . *Two* . . . What kind of life do you think you'll have? . . . *Three* . . . A sailor in the sky, drifting from port to port, utterly useless! . . . *Four* . . . Your mother would turn in her grave . . . *Five!* Thank you

Attaining Belief in Yourself

very much, the nail in the proverbial coffin! Though they'd been overused by a father conniving to get his way, those words had a powerful effect on Pierce. He had lost his mother long before establishing any understanding of what she expected, if anything, of her younger son. Manipulation on his father's part, while unfair, did not matter to Pierce; even the slightest hint of his mother's disapproval had always forced him to rethink his direction.

As the candles burned down to tiny pools of molten wax, the scent of incense long gone, Pierce's eyes began to feel heavy with sleep. One poem in particular stood out from the book he'd selected. It was called "Once You're Gone," and was a most timely piece, given the soul-searching purpose of his journey to Colorado. Despite his aching body's urge to sleep, he read it one more time, before drifting off into a deep slumber, reflecting on his own path.

Once You're Gone

Once you're gone, who will remember your smile?
Who will honor your legacy and say it was worthwhile
to know and love you while you were here?
Who will miss and remember you year after year?
And given the chance, once you depart,
to glance over your shoulder and
reflect on your time
will you look back with sadness
and a tinge of regret
for the things you recall
or the things you forget?
The color of money, or a star-kissed sky
the ink on your bank statements, or your child's blue eyes?

The person who wronged you, or the person who loved
what will you see when you look back from above?
The path you have walked from the day you were born
led to this place, turn around take a look
Do you see your own footprints
or a path that's well worn?
Did you lead or follow?
Pioneer or bleep?
Blaze the trail or baa like a sheep?
Did people hang on every wise word
or did you hold back, follow the herd?
Would it matter to you if it were long or short
if the prints left behind stood proud and alone?
Could you look back with pride
at the difference you made
with your time on this earth
and the path that you paved?
Tracing that path to the lives you have touched
when you look back, is your heart filled with love?
Do you see friends and loved ones
or a sad, empty trail?
Did you make an impact
or does your path ail?
A strong imprint of a life well lived
or the faded memory of a wasted gift?
When your name comes up, do they smile or yawn?
How will you be remembered, once you're gone?

■ ■ ■

Pierce awoke early, side-swiped momentarily by that awkward, uneasy feeling familiar to travelers when one waits for

37

Attaining Belief in Yourself

the mind to catch up with the body, relaying the story of how it came to be where it now rested. Behind the golden Buddha, stretching beyond the wall of glass as far as his eyes could see, bristlecone pines, spruces, and Douglas firs shivered in the wind, their weighted branches glistening silver-white. Four to five feet of untouched snow, pristine and pure, piled against the glass, as the wind whipped fresh, falling flakes, whirling them in circles, not allowing them to touch the ground, like a child playing a game.

Pain showed no mercy, quickly stealing the pleasure of this view from him. Memory followed fast, filling in the gaps of how he—isolated and injured—had gained audience to such magnificence.

Moving slowly, carefully, he reached for the twisted staff and hobbled along, wincing in pain as he fumbled and accidentally put weight on the wrong leg, finding his way to the living area in search of Jon. Surely, *he* owned a cellular phone that actually worked out here.

A teapot and cups sat invitingly on the slate countertop that marked the beginning of the kitchen, and was the only sign of life. Cautiously synchronizing the movements between his splinted leg and the walking stick, Pierce managed to cross the room. He arrived at the counter and poured a cup of tea as a reward for his effort. As he sipped the tasty brew, he watched as the storm cavorted outside, feeling like he was sitting inside a snow globe. Catching a rapid movement in his peripheral vision, he turned to find Jon, poised and motionless, a bizarre abstract human sculpture.

Jon, it appeared, was tied in a knot.

He was positioned at the center of an all-glass room perpendicular to the living area that jutted out into the wilderness. His legs hovered in mid-air, splitting in opposite directions, like a pair of scissors. Defying gravity, he held them there, level with his shoulders and torso, which appeared to be balancing on his triceps and elbows. His two hands, planted firmly on the floor, were the only part of his body not suspended in the air. Pierce watched for an eternity, as Jon stayed there, unflinching, frozen in time. Then suddenly, without warning, he moved, smoothly jumping into a low push-up position, his entire body hovering two inches off the ground. Again, he held this position for a painfully long time. Finally pressing into his hands, he lifted his entire body up, swinging his legs and torso like a pendulum under the arch-like bridge forged by his arms and shoulders. Back and forth, back and forth, back and forth . . . Pierce was blown away by this incredible display of strength.

The impressive gymnastics continued for a good 30 minutes, when Jon finally joined Pierce at the counter. "Ah, you found the tea."

"Strength training?" Pierce asked, gesturing toward the glass room Jon had come from.

"Close," he smiled. "Yoga." Eyeing the staff, he nodded. "I see you found my magic stick. How do you feel this morning?"

"Okay, considering." He watched as Jon slowly, deliberately wrapped his fingers around the steaming cup of tea he poured for himself. Raising it to his face, he breathed in the aroma of tea and closed his eyes, savoring the moment as he lingered there. Puzzled, Pierce wondered if Jon actually drank tea or simply breathed its vapors.

Attaining Belief in Yourself

Jon opened his eyes. "You must be hungry. Shall I fix us some breakfast?"

Pierce observed Jon with a mild curiosity as he set about the kitchen with purposeful movement, opening cabinets, drawers, even jars as if they were intricately wrapped gifts. Mindfully taking one egg at a time from a basket on the countertop, he cracked them open, barely making a sound, draining the viscous fluids into a mixing bowl, artfully grinding in pepper and salt before adding some dried herbs. It looked more like a choreographed dance than a man whipping up a quick breakfast.

"Gas." He smiled at Pierce as he fired up the stovetop. "My architect's idea. I wanted electric appliances throughout, didn't want to mess with venting issues, pilot lights, and the like. He won. Talked me into a gas hot water system too. Times like these, I'm glad I listened to him."

"When do you expect to get power back?"

"Couple of days . . . after the blizzard passes."

Jon put two placemats, two plates, forks, and knives and a neat stack of sliced bread on the countertop near where Pierce sat.

He then turned wordlessly and headed outside. A sharp, bitter cold sliced the air as Jon slid the door open. Pierce watched him take a few steps before digging at something in the snow. Closing the door behind him, Jon padded back to the kitchen, placing a tub of ice-cold butter and a frozen pint of orange juice on the counter. Pierce tried to laugh but his swollen face would not allow it.

"Thank you for breakfast, and your kind hospitality," Pierce said in between bites of the surprisingly tasty scramble.

Jon silently chewed what was in his mouth, carefully swallowing before responding. "You're very welcome." Pierce noted the time Jon took to taste and savor each bite, and made a conscious effort to slow down too. He wasn't eating quite as slowly as Jon, but he was no longer shoveling the food in. He had to admit, it tasted better.

"I noticed my cell phone doesn't receive a signal here. I was hoping I could use yours?" Pierce inquired hopefully.

Jon shook his head. "I don't bring my cell phone when I come out here."

Pierce was dumbfounded. Reading his shocked expression, Jon added, "If anybody really needs me, I've got the landline. Shame that's not gas too, in this situation." He laughed, eyeing the cordless phone sitting dead in its cradle.

Blatantly irresponsible! What if there was an emergency? Like an accident? Pierce asked himself ironically—and idiotically.

Staring out into the blustery, untamed wilderness, Pierce felt like a fool, fighting something he had absolutely no control over. The weather. Ignorantly blaming Jon's lifestyle for being stranded without a phone or electricity bore no logic either. How could he fault Jon, when it was he who plowed through the fence? The fire popped in the living room, drawing Pierce's attention back to that part of the house. Draped in elegant serenity, it really was a beautiful home.

"No TV?" Pierce observed. Catching the accusing edge in his voice, he strived to understand why he was being hypercritical of this man's lifestyle. Other than being temporarily stuck in his world, how Jon chose to live had very little

Attaining Belief in Yourself

to do with Pierce. Yet, here he sat, judging him. And harshly, too.

"No TV." Jon slowly stacked the dishes, taking them to the sink. "We couldn't watch right now anyway," he added with a chuckle.

Unable to determine whether he was more irritated or intrigued by this man, Pierce knew one thing for sure: He would lose his mind if he chose to live this way. He was immediately struck with an irrational fear of Jon's hermetic habits rubbing off on him, and he excused himself from Jon's company to try to take a shower.

As the spacious, natural stone bathroom filled with steam, Pierce inspected his battered, bruised face in the mirror. It looked a lot worse than it felt. Stale brown blood clotted in beads, framing the gash across his brow, resembling a dried up zipper. He imagined opening that zipper and reaching deep within, removing the things he did not like about himself—things revealed during his short time here with Jon. Without distraction, forced to bear witness to his behavior and shortcomings, he realized that he truly did not like the person unfolding before him. Freshly examining his selfish attempts to blame others—Jon, Sarah, even Anderson—for his problems exposed hints of unfairness and downright senselessness. In spite of the accident, he certainly was attaining a lot of insight.

Then he thought about it a moment longer, and corrected himself. Perhaps the "accident" was no accident at all—and his chance meeting with Jon was in fact a valuable gift.

■ ■ ■

The two men sat by the fire, observing the finally yielding storm. Freshly showered, and feeling much more relaxed, Pierce had his leg elevated on cushions, an ice compress stuffed with fresh snow securely bandaged to his injured knee. Jon's coaxing had led Pierce to share a little information about his company, and Sarah's request for him to take time out from it—and everything else. Turning to Jon, he asked, "So what do *you* do, Jon? You some kind of self-help guru?"

Jon laughed heartily as he moved to stoke the fire with more wood. "A guru at helping myself, yes, but I'm afraid it ends there." He chuckled to himself, evidently getting a huge kick out of Pierce's question.

Taking up residence on his floor cushion once again, Jon fell into silent meditation. Pierce shifted in his seat, feeling awkward, like an intruder caught in someone else's private moment. Opening his eyes, Jon reached for and began fondly caressing the "magic stick"—turning it over and over in his hands, seemingly admiring the craftsmanship. For the first time, Pierce recognized the knots and twists in the gnarly thing to be birds, snakes, and fish. A weird and wonderful menagerie, intricately and skillfully carved to form a magical piece of art. He could also see that Jon was thousands of miles away.

An eternity seemed to pass before Jon finally spoke. "I have a story to tell, if you'll humor me." Taking the silence as his cue, he continued. "I was very much like you once, Pierce. On the fast track, wildly successful in business . . . successful beyond comprehension."

Pierce tried to speak, but Jon silenced him.

Attaining Belief in Yourself

"In you, I see my *old* self . . . one hand hovering over the self-destruct button . . . " He trailed off, lost in thought. "You asked if I was a self-help guru. No, I'm not. But I have been blessed with great teachers, and great lessons masquerading as harsh falls. And I know that you don't need to suffer as I once did. You don't need to press that button, my friend. The choice is yours."

Jon appeared to be rambling, and Pierce was confused. His mind shifted gears swiftly, trying to make sense of the situation. Was Jon's controlled, calm demeanor simply a mask for complete, utter lunacy?

Leaving Pierce alone, Jon disappeared down the hall. Pierce panicked, desperately searching for a knife or heavy, blunt object—*anything* he could use in self-defense. From the end hall, he heard a toilet flushing. In a race against time, Pierce eyed the heavy, empty vase on the coffee table. Testing his reach, he carefully repositioned himself closer to it. When Jon returned, Pierce noticed he was also armed— with Pierce's copy of *Success!* magazine.

Slowly placing the magazine on the coffee table, moving the vase to one side, Jon returned to his floor cushion and watched in mild amusement as Pierce made the connection.

Looking from the glossy cover, back to Jon, back to the cover, back to Jon, and finally back to the cover, the cogwheels in Pierce's mind whirred, while the gears shifted once again, crunching away. None of this made sense. Pierce sat with his mouth gaping open.

"I'm Jon Davis."

"The man behind BBA Health," Pierce finished for him, barely whispering, "celebrating four-plus years at Forbes

#12." Switching the monk costume out for the power-suit, the man who sat before him and the one staring out from the glossy cover were, indeed, interchangeable. Pierce was at once embarrassed. Humbled. Awed. Any concerns and complaints he had of snowstorms and failed electricity idled somewhere, far, far away.

Questions spewed forward, yet when he tried to speak, Pierce faltered. "You own a Fortune 500 company and you're meditating in a blizzard in the middle of Colorado . . . are you insane?" He finally blurted out.

"Pierce, I would be insane if I *did not* retreat here." The warm smile that had, only yesterday, pissed Pierce off, returned. "I'm hungry. What do you think about lunch?"

Pierce laughed at the irony. One of the country's most successful business leaders wanted to fix *him* lunch. He laughed even harder as he pictured Jon dragging his dead weight through a blizzard . . . on a snowmobile! And harder still, at the idea of Jon washing him up and changing his clothes, like a mother bathing a young child coming in from a rough play-date. His swollen face objected to the movement, but he didn't care—he laughed through the pain until tears flowed down his cheeks. He finally composed himself and joined Jon in the kitchen, assuming his position on the stool at the counter. He watched as Jon pieced together lunch.

Turning a can of corn in his hands, Jon admitted, "I loathe canned vegetables. I eat fresh as a rule, but given the weather can change on a dime out here, I keep my pantry stocked with these little gems, canned vegetables."

"How long have you lived out here, Jon?"

"Well, let's see. I've owned this place for over 15 years. I initially built it as a party pad, but as I grew, so it did, into my private retreat. I don't live here per se, but I do spend every other month here."

Pierce is mortified. "Without a cell phone?"

Jon shrugged. "My secretary and my girlfriend are the only two people who know the landline number. I trust their judgment if they need to use it. Otherwise, yes; I prefer to remain incommunicado while here."

"But—the snowstorm? Your landline is out? What if they needed you now? A major business decision, like a merger or some such." Pierce's stomach flipped, lurching into his chest the minute the word *merger* crossed his lips. He had forgotten an extremely important meeting that had been scheduled for this coming Monday. Distracted, he tried to focus on what Jon was saying.

Jon set the can opener down on the counter. "Pierce, I believe in the people I hired to run my company as much as I believe in myself. I sit on the board of directors, and, while I am there every other month to oversee things, it all runs very smoothly when I spend time here. I actually think it operates much *better* without me breathing down their necks, micromanaging."

This struck a chord with Pierce. He wondered if he could relinquish control to somebody like Anderson. In just a few days, he feared the worse for his company. Doubts had plagued him well before departing from Charlotte, and he felt physically ill at the notion of missing Monday's meeting. Praying the power would return sooner so he could call to postpone the meeting—or at least teleconference to sit in on

46

it—Pierce knew he could never be as relaxed as Jon with another person at the helm of all he had worked so hard to build. Never! How did Jon have such trust and faith in people?

As though reading his thoughts, Jon asked, "Do you trust the people you hired to do their jobs well, Pierce?" He turned back to his cooking while Pierce wrestled with the loaded question. Answering no would indicate he failed by hiring poorly, whereas yes meant that he failed by not letting go. Whichever it was, he had ended up here—stressed out and overworked. And it was clear that he, and only he, was 100 percent responsible for the state he was in.

Sensing Pierce's frustration, Jon added, "Pierce, you told me earlier that you employ over 600 people. You can't be micromanaging them all; that's physically impossible! Somebody—several people, in fact—in your management team must be doing *something* right, or you would have gone under long ago."

Pierce swallowed hard. He hoped Jon was right. If he could not get ahold of Anderson before 9:00 AM EST the following day, then the possibility of expanding his company into Middle Eastern and Asian markets—via a subcontracting agreement with a major Indian technology company called Nabhas—rested solely on Anderson's shoulders. Pinching his eyes closed, Pierce began to breathe slowly and deliberately, willing the nausea and doubts to subside. If only he had checked his calendar more closely, or synched his BlackBerry with his work calendar last Thursday before leaving the office, he'd have caught this error before touching down in Denver.

Easing his eyes open, Pierce resigned himself to a cold, hard fact: This situation was beyond his control. His only hope was the electricity returning in time—the earlier the better. Turning his attention back to his host, he listened as Jon moved toward Pierce, pulled up the second stool, and took a seat.

"About 16 years ago, I was at the top of my game. The health insurance business I'd built from scratch was rated as the largest in the country. I believed I was invincible.

"And then my wife left me. Filed for divorce. 'Irreconcilable differences.'" He let this linger, marinate, before asking Pierce, "Sound familiar?"

"I had no idea what those 'differences' were, since I hardly spent any time with her by that point. It was all work, or play—no marriage. She hired a divorce attorney who dragged the battle through the mud for almost a year. Giving her half of the company's value would have sent me to the doghouse. So, out of spite—and desperate to end an ugly divorce—I sold it. Even giving her half its value allowed me to maintain my wild lifestyle. Only this time, I had nobody grounding me. Private jets, yachts, wild parties, hopping from city to city . . . I played hard. I was hurt, angry, and desperately insecure, and turned to drugs. Oh, sure, I believed I was untouchable, a cocky bastard living the life. But in reality, I was nothing more than scared and lonely." Jon rose, walking slowly to the stove; he stirred the rice as it tempestuously gurgled and spat over the medium flame. He lowered it to a simmer.

"I splurged on this property and several others after paying out Blair, my ex-wife, and partied for a good solid year. Then one day, about 14 years ago, I woke in a gutter on a dirty street in Rio de Janeiro. I'd been mugged, but I had also been out of it for days, high on a four-day bender."

Pierce couldn't believe his ears. Or eyes. The person Jon described did not remotely fit the image that stood before him.

"Looking back, I am deeply ashamed of my behavior— my unreasonable angst at the world, and the way I treated people, including myself. A dear and trusted friend in Rio helped me get back on my feet after the bender. He offered me a place to sleep while I replaced my credit cards and obtained a new passport from the embassy. During my stay, he encouraged me to commit to a 'spiritual' kind of rehab.

"I knew something had to change at this point. I was 49 years old and running wild like a 20-year-old. Regaining consciousness, face down, in that filthy gutter was definitely my lowest point—*and* my turning point. I didn't just regain consciousness that day; I *woke up!* And once I caught a glimpse of the possibility of who I could be—instead of what I had become—I wasted no time pursuing it."

Tossing the cooked rice into a wok full of sautéed vegetables, Jon added soy sauce and seasoning before dividing the bounty between two plates. Pierce watched, amazed. Even relaying his own dramatic story, Jon remained even-keeled, moving mindfully and gracefully across the kitchen, preparing lunch. It wasn't that he lacked passion; he had simply developed a level of detachment. He exhibited an uncanny refusal to carry negative emotion from his past forward, and he had told his story in a matter-of-fact manner, unperturbed by any disturbing memories. "Onward and

Attaining Belief in Yourself

upward," Pierce reflected, once again; his father's method for dealing with life changes was a very different approach from Jon's—and one Pierce feared he erred toward in his own life. Jon, it appeared, *processed* what he experienced before moving forward with a nonjudgmental *acceptance*, using the lesson to facilitate change and to become greater. It was formidable to be in this man's presence.

As they ate, Pierce noticed with a twinge of regret that the snow, grown tired of her game, had completely surrendered. The afternoon sun beamed brightly through icy trees. Pulsing rays of golden-white light bounced off the glistening pine needles, glittering like stars, a sparkling kaleidoscope of silver and gold. Pierce understood that this dazzling scene signaled his time with Jon would soon be drawing to a close, and he urged him to go on. "Your story, Jon . . . How long were you in rehab? When . . . How did you return to corporate life?"

Chewing slowly, Jon placed his fork beside his plate. Staring out beyond the picturesque scene, he continued to chew his food unhurriedly, fully present. Pierce wanted to shake the man! Any patience he had demonstrated for these deliberate gestures had vanished. *Not now!* Time was limited! He knew that these were traits he needed to learn from Jon, most likely a large link in the chain to his success. But in this moment, Pierce wanted more than anything for Jon to lose all restraint and tell him everything he could; not in between long, laborious bites, but right now—with his mouth full! He wanted this man to passionately unload every tidbit he had . . . pour out every valuable lesson, every tip, every secret. Any advice he could offer, Pierce wanted to drink up greedily.

Unlike his earlier, irrational fear of Jon's hermetic tendencies rubbing off on him, Pierce clung to the hope that the business savvy and wisdom of this heavy-hitter would be highly contagious.

"So beautiful out," Jon finally spoke. "Perhaps, if you are feeling up to it, we'll take the snowmobile out this afternoon. Take stock of the damage to your vehicle. I believe it is totaled, but you might want to see for yourself."

The rental? Who cared about the stupid rental? Pierce thought. "Jon, I would really love to hear the rest of your story."

But Jon had already picked up his fork. Pierce sighed, knowing it would be a very long time between bites.

■ ■ ■

Night fell fast on the sleepy retreat. Just before dusk, Pierce begrudgingly assessed the damaged Suzuki, and, as expected, Jon had been correct in his judgment: It was totaled. Once the power was restored, he'd gladly call the rental company to report the accident, happily allowing the crumpled mess to become their problem. He longed to call Sarah and hear her voice, along with Lila's and Max's. Oddly, his anxieties about Blackbird Tech had dissipated; while he still wanted to check in and hoped to teleconference in on the meeting with Nabhas, the burning desire for control had tempered a little as he loosened his grip on the reins.

Yes, the return of power would be a gift. Now walking better—albeit with Jon's cane—Pierce was uncertain what he would do when it came time to relieve Jon of his presence.

51

Attaining Belief in Yourself

Would he continue on to the lodge at Woodland Park, or return home to lick his wounds? Fear of yet another snowstorm had him leaning toward the latter.

Lost in his own thoughts, he did not notice Jon slip into the room; the aroma of freshly brewed tea eventually roused him back to the present. Pouring a cup for Pierce, Jon broke the silence. "Power should be back tomorrow evening, the morning after at the latest." As always, it seemed, Jon had accessed his thoughts.

"Today is Sunday. I must return to Oregon later this week to fulfill my duties on the board. Thursday, most likely. You don't have to rush off, Pierce, if you don't want to. You are welcome to stay on until then."

"Thank you." Pierce accepted the tea, but the gratitude expressed ran much deeper.

Jon closed his eyes, enjoying the wafting aroma from the steaming mug he held in both hands. Pierce tried it too, gently wrapping both hands around the large clay mug; he rested his lips on the smoothly glazed edge and breathed deeply, slowly. He was amazed to discover that time appeared to stand still. Nothing existed beyond the warm sensation that crept into his hands and caressed his face, along with the slightly bitter aroma of tea. All other sensation, all other thought, melted away, a mini, yet powerful meditation.

Catching him, Jon laughed softly, "Ah, you just learned my greatest secret." Opening his eyes, slightly embarrassed at being sprung, Pierce shot him a quizzical look.

"Do you honestly believe a high-strung, middle-aged man, binging on cocaine and booze just plopped down one day and disappeared into a long, soulful meditation?" Jon laughed. "No, no, no . . . my guru, my wonderful guru, Sosanna . . ." Jon smiled at her memory. "She started me off slowly, incrementally. Cautious, tender, baby steps."

"Crawling before running," Pierce offered.

"Exactly," Jon said before both men turned back to their tea and gently closed their eyes.

"Tell me about her . . . your guru." Pierce asked after several beats. Studying Jon's face, illuminated by the burning fire, he looked young for, by Pierce's calculation, his 63 years. And incredibly fit.

Jon's eyes misted over. There was a side of the man Pierce had yet to see; it was clear this woman meant the world to him.

Slowly, Jon reached for the magic stick. "Sosanna," he smiled, turning the stick in his hands. "This belonged to her, you know? A medicine man in her village near Lago Atitlan, Guatemala, fashioned it for her. The animals represented, native to the lake, are said to ward off evil spirits. Not the external kind, but the invisible ones we wrestle within our own hearts and minds."

As Pierce patiently waited for Jon to continue, shadows from the fire flickered, lapping at his face.

"Sosanna was no different from me when she arrived in Central America, washed up, stoned, and empty. After many years roaming lost, she was embraced by a Mayan tribe and finally felt she belonged somewhere. She'd been orphaned and alone for more than 10 years, and the tribe's uncondi-tional love and support gave Sosanna the strength to draw on her difficult past—and even on the struggles of ancestors long buried. It gave her a way to rebuild a new path for herself, and in doing so, she discovered how *she* could help others. She often claimed that if her chance meeting with the Mayans hadn't occurred, she would have died of an overdose." He stared deep into the crackling fire.

"Thirty years on, when I stumbled into the same village—tired, weary, and heartbroken—she feared much the same for me. By this time, Sosanna had built quite a reputation for herself; many a lost soul found their way to Lago Atitlan in search of this heavily wrinkled, wise woman. People were eager to place their very last hopes of beating out their demons in her hands." Jon waved the magic stick—the conqueror of demons.

"With this very stick in her hands, Sosanna and I fell into the habit of taking long evening strolls by the majestic lake. As I learned about her life, a stark contrast to my own privileged past, I found myself filled with deep, unsettling feelings of shame and regret. I knew I could be better, believed it to my core, and, with Sosanna's guidance, I maintained that belief; after about a year at the lake I was strong enough to return to Portland."

Pierce poured more tea. "What happened when you returned?"

"I ran into Blair during my first week home. She had remarried some uber-wealthy Silicon Valley investor who snobbishly praised my common sense in selling the company, given it was about to go completely under. I was heartbroken that something I had worked so hard to build was dying. So the following day, I placed all of the properties that I owned on the market and rented a cheap, austere studio apartment in Portland. I made a meager bid on my old company, and regained control. Slowly and methodically I set out to rebuild it, maintaining the values Sosanna instilled in me."

"Do you keep in touch with Sosanna?" Pierce asked, entertaining the hope of meeting her himself one day.

"She died two years ago. I flew back to the Atitlan one last time to read her eulogy. Even in death she gifted me, the honor to tell her story and celebrate her life . . . and this old thing." He marveled at the stick one more time before banging it into the hardwood floor, startling Pierce.

Stiff, sore, and tired, Pierce realized he had been listening to Jon for hours. He asked Jon for more painkillers before retiring to bed. He was hungry—for food and to learn more about Jon's and Sosanna's methods—and vowed to probe Jon further the following day.

■ ■ ■

Once again, Pierce awoke early. Watching the sun pushing the heavy darkness aside, he lay perfectly still as a deer and her fawn broke through the thick wilderness and sniffed around the snow outside the glass wall. The innocence and grace of these beautiful animals made him think of his children. Happiness washed over him, knowing there was a possibility of calling home today if the power returned.

He reached for the stick and saw it now in a new light, a powerful symbol of two triumphant journeys and the forging of an unlikely, enduring friendship. He felt honored that Jon had allowed him to use it. Crossing to the bathroom to brush his teeth, he wondered if he and Jon would remain friends. He certainly hoped so.

Attaining Belief in Yourself

Pouring a mug of tea in the kitchen, Pierce practiced the tea meditation, sneaking peaks at Jon's powerful yoga routine in between. Baby steps, he thought to himself, grateful that his knee injury offered him the perfect excuse not to try yoga.

Joining Pierce, Jon placed the magazine in front of him. Tapping its cover for emphasis, he said, "In honor of Sosanna, I agreed to the *Success!* interview. I know it may seem an unlikely vehicle for her methods, but it is not only junkies who get lost. Many people in the corporate sphere lose their way too. I'd fallen from grace in both worlds when she came into my life. She's the one who helped me build what I have now. Her methods *are* the core to my success today, and it is my duty to share them with others."

A keen and eager student, Pierce rapidly flipped through the magazine searching for the article—a full feature on Jon and BBA Health—followed by a boxed section laying out Sosanna's five-step exercise: *Attaining Belief in Yourself*. A boldface quote from Jon segued the exercise:

To be a great leader, you must trust in others. To trust in others, you must attain belief in others. To attain belief in others, you must first attain belief in yourself.

—Jon Davis, Founder and CEO, BBA Health

"Pierce, I cannot do the soul-searching for you. Only you can do that. But I can offer you the tools." Jon gestured toward the magazine. "There are many things I need to take care of before we leave Thursday; this will give you space to work on yourself in solitude. Of course, if you need me, you will find me." He padded off toward a staircase beyond the living area, before turning and adding, "I plan to leave at 7:30 AM Thursday, and I can drop you at Denver airport then."

As Jon disappeared up the stairs, a light flickered above Pierce's head, a playful hint that the electricity might soon awaken. Pierce glanced up in hopeful anticipation as the light overhead winked at him, blinking one last time before falling dark and silent. He waited, but nothing happened. Picking up his mug of tea, he read Jon's article from start to finish. He could not help but wonder where the mysterious man had gone off too. Surely he would see him at mealtimes, or at breakfast doing his yoga.

Over the next two days, the only trace of Jon came in the form of meals left out for Pierce to enjoy, and freshly brewed tea waiting on the counter each morning. Although deeply puzzled by Jon's unconventional ways, Pierce seized the opportunity to begin his inner journey. He also began working through the exercises that Jon had essentially sworn by. Delving right in, exploring his strengths and weaknesses, it quickly became evident that two days would not be enough time to complete this work properly. When the power finally kicked in, energizing the retreat with a glowing hum, he anxiously waited for Jon's cordless landline to recharge. It was Tuesday evening. He'd long surrendered the opportunity of teleconferencing the meeting, but he had not spoken to Sarah since he left Charlotte. The phone could not charge fast enough.

"Pierce?" Sarah asked, her voice a blend of relief and joy.

"Hi, honey."

"Wh-at . . . where are you?"

Attaining Belief in Yourself

"Safe. I—" He sighed heavily, knowing she would freak out when he told her about the accident. "First and foremost I am okay, I had a little bit of an accid-"

"Accident? Are you okay?"

"Absolutely fine. My knee is twisted and sprained, but other than that . . . well, actually, it's all been a really interesting experience." Sarah remained silent. "Sarah, there was a huge snowstorm here and the power's been down for days. I tried to reach you, but I'm in the middle of nowhere with no signal. I am so sorry if you were worried."

"I was. The lodge . . . I called them two days ago to check in with you and they told me you never made it. Pierce, I have been beside myself. The police told me to wait, that a large band of the state had power outages and you were most likely safely waiting it out somewhere . . . but, well, you can imagine how frustrating it has been to just wait."

"Believe me, I do." He smiled at the irony. "It's good to hear your voice. How are the kids?"

"They're great. They had no idea—they think you're off on a business trip."

"Well, in a way, I guess I am. Everything else okay at home?"

"Now that I know you are safe? Of course! Yes, everything is fine." She trailed off. "Pierce, I am so sorry to put you in this situation. If I had not pushed you . . ."

"Sssshhh. You have no idea. The busted knee and accident I could have done without, of course, but it led me to meet an amazing person. I've been staying in his retreat and it's been quite an extraordinary experience. So much more so than if I'd stayed in the mountain lodge on my own." It was now Sarah's turn to laugh at the irony. And once she started, she could not stop; Pierce joined her until there were tears rolling down both of their cheeks.

"I'm glad it worked out," she finally caught her breath to speak, "and I'm glad you're okay, Pierce. I was so scared, and guilt ridden, that I forced you out there to stumble into a terrible fate."

"Well, you did. But my fate's been quite amazing so far." He could feel her smiling down the line. "Sarah?"

"Yes?"

"My host is leaving on Thursday, heading back to Oregon. I feel like I need more time to work on myself."

"You want to stay?" She could hardly believe her ears.

"Well, I considered continuing on to the lodge, but I really don't want to chance another snowstorm. I'm kind of thinking of heading somewhere else, just for a few days."

"Where?"

"Not sure yet."

"So long as you feel okay, you should stay away as long as you need to . . . but, Pierce?"

"Yes?"

"Please, please, check in with me every couple of days. I don't want to go through what I did the last couple of days— ever again."

"You got it."

"I'm really proud of you. Taking this journey."

"You putting the kids to bed soon?"

"As soon as I get off the phone."

"Give them the biggest hug and kiss from me. I'll speak to them next time I call, don't want to wind them up before bed.

Attaining Belief in Yourself

I'll call you in a couple of days when I know where I am heading."

"Good night, my love."

Returning the phone to its cradle, Pierce stared at it for the longest time. Good night, he finally said to the cool evening air. Refilling his tea, he sat and pondered where he should go next.

When Thursday arrived, Pierce wheeled his luggage out to the living area where he found Jon, sitting in an actual chair for once, dressed smartly in designer jeans and a crewneck sweater. Pierce almost did not recognize him without the monk attire. Letting go of his luggage, Pierce stumbled a little as he stepped toward Jon, who leapt from his seat to catch him, "Steady! You okay? Where is your magic stick?"

"In the guest room, where I found it."

Smiling, Jon disappeared momentarily before returning with the stick.

"Please, I want you to take this."

"I—I, I couldn't," Pierce protested, knowing the item's immeasurable sentimental value.

Placing one hand on Pierce's shoulder, Jon eased the stick into his hand. "I want you to keep this, Pierce. Let it be a symbol of our time together, of the journey you are embarking on."

Pierce was lost for words. Draping his arm across Pierce's shoulders, Jon picked up the luggage with his free hand before adding, "You need it much more than I do right now," politely nodding toward Pierce's injured leg. Pierce understood that Jon was referring to the stick's mystical qualities more so than its practical ones.

Own YOUR Success

After making most of the drive in comfortable, silent meditation, Jon dropped Pierce at Denver airport. Pierce gripped Jon in a tight bear hug before saying goodbye, and was once again at a loss for words. He sighed heavily and released Jon from his grip. "Jon, I will never forget you. Your kind hospitality, your generosity. I can't thank you enough for all you have given me. I hope our paths cross again one day soon."

The two men hugged one last time. "Good luck, Pierce. Enjoy the journey." Jon waved as he drove off toward the private airport, where his small private jet was housed.

Pierce was inspired by Jon's story and revved up for the next part of his journey. He acknowledged that while he did not harbor idealistic fantasies of meeting a Sosanna, he certainly hoped to dig deep enough to come face to face with himself. Hobbling to the ticket counter, he purchased a ticket to San Diego. He had a couple of hours to kill before the flight would depart, so he first called Sarah, and then Anderson, to check in.

"Where are you off to?" Sarah asked, as excited for this experience as Pierce was.

"Sunny San Diego." He smiled into the cracked phone, reminding himself to have the device replaced once he reached his destination.

"San Diego? Well, at least you won't get snowed in there!"

"That's the plan." He laughed. "Thank you, Sarah."

"For what?"

"You know what." He smiled. God, he missed her.

"No problem. Travel safe."

Pierce's next call was to the Blackbird Tech offices. He had already reviewed the minutes of Monday's meeting, and

Attaining Belief in Yourself

the newly negotiated contract with Nabhas that Nora e-mailed to him on Wednesday. Pierce was impressed with Anderson's ability to work closely with Blackbird Tech's legal team to negotiate an agreement beyond Pierce's wildest dreams. Anderson more than nailed Pierce's expectations for this deal—he surpassed them! Swallowing his pride, Pierce dialed Anderson.

"Anderson."

"Anderson. Pierce. I hear things are still standing without me there." Pierce listened as Anderson's hearty laugh echoed down the line.

"Pierce. How are you? Yes, things are still standing—a little wobbly, of course, but still standing. I was a little surprised you did not teleconference on Monday. I know how important nabbing the Nabhas contract was to you."

"No. I knew the Nahbas deal was in capable hands," he lied. "Congratulations, by the way, on a marvelous job."

"Thanks. They fought to the end, but I wasn't giving in until we had that deal on *our* terms."

"Could not have done it better myself," Pierce said lightly, yet deep down, he knew it was true.

"So, when are you back?" Anderson asked, sincerely curious.

"In a week or so. You good holding the fort until then?"

"Of course I am. We have a good team here—it's all under control." Pierce smiled, as a comment Jon had made about his management team came to mind.

"Well, once again, congratulations. Appreciate your hard work. I'll see you soon."

"Thanks, Pierce. Bye."

Own YOUR Success

As he hung up the phone Pierce reluctantly admitted, to himself, that the negotiation may *not* have been as successful had he been there. He was beginning to understand how Jon's management strategy worked—and after witnessing how this kind of teamwork and trust in action on the part of his own employees had garnered amazing results, Pierce allowed himself to relax a little more. Retrieving his journal and the copy of *Success!* from his luggage, Pierce sank deep into the large black leather seat to review Sosanna's exercises.

Five Key Factors for Attaining Belief in Yourself

1. *Accept the truth:* Realizing and identifying with the person you are today is the key to becoming the person you want to be. We never actually *fail* in life; we just don't always get the results that we want. You have to acknowledge and identify with what is most important in your life and, ultimately, "Attain Belief in Yourself."

2. *Speak the truth:* The regret you feel from your past behavior and habits may cause you to feel terrified about acknowledging or discussing them. However, this reluctance to face the past only amplifies the pain and makes us feel like victims. Get the truth out into the light. Talk about your experience with a trusted friend or a professional.

3. *Breathe through the truth:* Even though every fiber of your being wants to react and believe that your actions up to this point have been correct, know that you can

change. Avoid acting from a place of pain or anger. The best way to reclaim your dignity is to act rationally and treat yourself lovingly. Do not self-destruct.

4. *Process the truth:* Give yourself time and space to find your equilibrium. Believe confidently and whole-heartedly that along with change you will develop a stronger foundation. Recognize that this will take time, and give yourself that time.

5. *Create a plan based on the truth:* Don't expect to be able to flip a switch and have a new, perfect life right away. Old behaviors and mind-sets often return. Stay strong and acknowledge that you must continue to believe and actively engage in this process to experience concrete change for your future. Define how you want to live your life from this point forward with this in mind.

Take out a piece of paper and write down any idea about the person you want to be and the life you want to live. Once you have clarity on this, you can take concrete steps toward realizing your goals and *Attaining Belief in Yourself.*

Chapter 4

Acting with Courage and Integrity

The Second Encounter

Courage is rightly esteemed the first of human qualities . . .
because it is the quality which guarantees all others.

—**Winston Churchill**

Armed with a fresh perspective, Pierce looked forward to spending some time in the sun to reflect. San Diego was an obvious choice for him, as it held many fond memories of summer vacations with his maternal grandparents as a young boy. Fresh air, sun, and sea were the perfect ingredients, providing a peaceful, tranquil backdrop for some serious introspection.

Sitting aboard the American Airlines craft, Pierce closed his eyes, honing his newfound meditation skills. Building on Jon's tea trick, he had graduated to seated meditations, managing up to 15 minutes in a given session. While his thoughts often drifted and the pain in his knee occasionally begged his consciousness for attention, his ability to focus improved with each session. Meditation began to play a major role in Pierce's day, and he felt as though he'd been rewarded with clarity for his perseverance. In fact, he questioned how he had lived without it. A typical knee-jerk reaction to issues would now be a thing of the past, as the tiny fracture in his mind slowly began to broaden. The sensation was palpable as Pierce's mind began its journey from closed to wide open, his heart following closely behind. Maturing buds, unfolding in the dawn light, stretched to their fullest potential.

"Excuse me, sir?" Pierce looked up. A tall, well-built man interrupted his internal sojourn. "May I?" He indicated the empty window seat next to Pierce.

"Of course." Pierce stood, allowing the gentleman passage to his assigned seat. How tall is this guy? he wondered, his eyes barely grazing the massive pectoral muscles squeezing by. He looked close to Pierce in age, about 42. Short, straw-colored hair, neatly clipped in a crew cut, coupled with the Navy SEAL emblem emblazoned on his polo, gave him away. Pierce offered his hand, "Pierce Edwards. Thank you for your service."

"Lieutenant J. Bobby Rehnquist." Gripping Pierce's hand, he added, "Pleased to meet you."

Pierce allowed the usual polite aircraft banter to ensue for 5 or 10 minutes before asking Lieutenant Rehnquist the burning question that was jumping up and down inside him like an excited, impatient child. From the moment he laid eyes on the SEAL insignia, boyhood fantasies of flying and battles flooding back, he was, by his own admission, in awe of this man. There had to be a great story or two stuffed up his sleeves next to those bulging biceps. As the plane reached cruising altitude, he turned to his neighbor and asked, "Lieutenant Rehnquist, what is it like? Being one of the elite? A Navy SEAL?"

A wry smile curled across Rehnquist's lightly freckled face. It was clear that he was asked this question often—perhaps *too* often.

"*Bobby*—please. I'm retired now," he responded. "Have been for several years. Oddly enough, I've been asked that question more in retirement than when I was serving."

Pierce was puzzled.

"Osama bin Laden." He allowed the name, and all atrocities attached to it, to linger, a foul and heavy stench clouding the air around them.

"SEAL applications surged following the capture and consequent death of bin Laden. Everybody wanted to be a SEAL, and those who did not, wanted to know one."

"Understandable," Pierce said.

"Oh, I agree. That mission certainly put our guys on the radar. Prior to that mission, however, people would thank me for my service, as you did, but rarely showed great interest in what we actually did."

"I'm sorry." Pierce felt embarrassed for having asked. "Are you saying the Osama bin Laden mission glorified the SEAL program?"

"In a way, yes. Yes it did."

Pierce struggled to think of something to say that might not offend Bobby—a new subject, or at least a different tangent.

"You know," Bobby went on, "people stop me in the street and congratulate me on bin Laden. Some want to shake my hand. And I wasn't even there! In fact, I was never part of Team Six when I *was* serving. I understand the sense of unified pride. We should all be proud of that mission—every man or woman serving, or retired, in all branches of the military, and each and every citizen. But it's still a very strange feeling being congratulated and thanked for something that you, unfortunately, did not play a role in."

"Unfortunately?"

"Oh yeah!" Bobby nodded enthusiastically. "That was a dream mission for any SEAL team member. Between you and me, I wish I could have been part of it!"

"You're saying that even though you've already completed your service, you would have come out of retirement for that one last mission?"

"Pierce, I would go back for *any* mission. While my service was a sacrifice, it was also a great honor. In fact, to this day, my greatest honor. I would do it all again if duty called. And yes, I would step out of retirement to fight for my country—without hesitation."

"Wow." Pierce was at a loss for words, suddenly aware that he had often taken for granted the sacrifice service women and men, and their families, make for his own safety and protection. Dedicating—many giving—their lives to provide freedom for all Americans. He began to think about all of the other relationships he took for granted, making a mental note to explore this in his journal once he arrived in San Diego.

Indicating the insignia on his breast, Bobby went on, "You see this?" Pinching his yellow shirt between his thumb and index finger, he pulled the shirt out so Pierce could get a good look at it. "Anchor represents the sea, eagle the air, and the pistol, the land. A Navy SEAL is highly trained to do battle in all areas—everybody knows this. But if you look closer, you will notice the pistol is cocked, signifying readiness for battle. And, see the eagle? The eagle's wings are spread wide, signifying courage and strength."

Bobby waited while Pierce studied the emblem. "In answer to your question, Pierce, that is what it is like to be a Navy SEAL. It is not glory. And, with a base salary of fifty-four thousand dollars per annum, it certainly is not dollars and cents. In a way, it goes beyond serving your country. It is courage and strength. It is integrity."

Pierce was profoundly ashamed. Fifty-four thousand dollars a year, an amount he usually averaged per paycheck and often more. Yet the biggest risk he took in his workday was driving on the expressway at peak hour. Remorsefully, he recalled an old, graying veteran standing outside his office near Memorial Day. Arthritic hands curled around the metal can he shook, requesting a donation of loose change as he offered Pierce a red poppy. Feeling pestered, Pierce brushed the old nuisance aside, rushing by him to a most important meeting. He now saw his actions as deplorable and unforgivable. Shame rippled through him, eating its way to the core of his cold, icy heart.

"Courage and integrity," Pierce repeated absentmindedly, his mind's eye fixed on the scene unfolding outside his office earlier that year. Vowing to make a generous donation to the Veterans Fund when he returned to Charlotte did little to alleviate his guilt. Not wanting to make the same mistake twice, he returned his full attention to the veteran seated beside him.

"How about the training? I've heard it is pretty intense."

Bobby laughed, "It certainly weeds out any wallflowers that may have slipped through. Want to hear a motto from SEAL training?"

69

Acting with Courage and Integrity

Pierce smiled encouragingly. Of course he did!

"The only easy day was yesterday."

Closing his eyes, allowing the words to penetrate deep within, Pierce rolled the motto around in his mind, chewing on it with great care. He liked it. He opened his eyes and turned to Bobby, encouraging him to go on.

"It takes a certain kind of person to complete the training. Courage and integrity comes from here," Bobby pointed to the middle of his chest, indicating his heart, "Many of those who recently rushed to apply for SEAL programs were going in with their ego. Ego is I. Team is we."

Pierce committed that to memory too. Bobby, it seemed, had many of these little gems to offer, Pierce began to understand he was in the presence of a truly great human being. Reclining his seat, he adjusted his splinted leg and relaxed as Bobby described SEAL training and the importance of teamwork in terms of survival.

"Brutal would be the best adjective to describe the more than 30 months of training a SEAL must complete before deployment. Those who do emerge from this training are ready to handle pretty much any task they could be called upon to perform—from diving, combat swimming or navigation, to demolitions, weapons, and parachuting. Pushed to the limit mentally and physically, the stresses endured during BUD/S training—"

"Buds?"

"Basic Underwater Demolition/SEAL. If trainees don't stand up to stressful situations simulated in training when lives are not at stake, chances are pretty good they'd be useless when lives *are* at stake! From day one, trainees learn the importance of teamwork. The focus is never on the individual. SEALS perform tasks that would be impossible for a single man to accomplish." He paused for effect. "It's all made possible by a team composed of highly qualified men sharing the same training and skills. Their success—*their survival*—depends on what they can achieve as a team. Survival is paramount to teamwork. The minute a link in the chain acts for himself, he puts dozens of others' lives at risk."

Pierce reflected on how this applied to his own line of work. Though lives were not at risk, dollars—and growth—certainly were. He was beginning to grasp the need to review his company's pyramid, beginning at the top. Perhaps he would scrub the idea of a pyramid altogether, in lieu of piecing together a highly skilled and capable team. Pierce's willingness to identify that more could be accomplished as a team was the direct effect of Bobby's formidable leadership skills.

"Bobby, I hope you realize that your training and background mean that you'd make a great leader. What is it you do now when you are retired from service?"

"Recruiting."

"For the SEALS?"

Bobby nodded, proudly.

"So, in a way, you *were* part of the team that captured Osama bin Laden."

Bobby laughed resignedly. "Yes, put that way, I guess you are correct."

"So, following all of the hype—how do you weed out the wannabes? It must be exhausting."

"Not really. They're usually quite transparent, with one eye trained on the mirror as they strut into my office.

71

Acting with Courage and Integrity

My technique is to *not* interview potential trainees—at least, not in the beginning. All of my recruiting begins with conversation. I encourage applicants to talk, and I merely listen. When too much chatter about Team Six arises—when I hear 'I did' instead of 'we did' in regards to prior military service—I encourage them to rethink their path. I would never dream of holding somebody back from chasing their beliefs and desires, but it is important that we figure out exactly why they are in our recruiting office. It's as crucial and beneficial to them as individuals as it is for our team. Pursuing the truth—exploring what drives you—takes great courage and integrity. While some of these young men leave my office without beginning a career as a SEAL, they *do* leave changed."

As the plane dipped, beginning its decent into San Diego, the ocean, cerulean and spectacular, came into view. It had been an interesting and enlightening 2 hours and 26 minutes for Pierce.

"Bobby—meeting you has been an unbelievable experience. Once again, I thank you for your service—not only to our country, but to those fortunate enough to cross your path. You truly are a formidable leader. Believe it or not, I've learned a lot from you myself. There are many changes I hope to implement within my own company by drawing on your SEAL experience. You've demonstrated how incredible an organization can be when its members work as a team, and how important it is to bring people together as opposed to focusing on their individual talents as I have always done. So, thank you."

Retrieving his luggage from the overhead bin, he shook Bobby's hand one last time. "If you ever tire of recruiting, you've got a big future in business and leadership consulting."

Turning, Pierce headed through the relatively quiet airport. Stepping through shiny glass sliding doors into the bright sunlight, he made his way to the taxi stand.

"Del Coronado Hotel," he instructed the driver before pulling his journal out, diligently making notes. There were three things Bobby had said that he did not want to forget.

Ego is I. Team is we.

The only easy day was yesterday.

Act with courage and integrity.

Completing the third note, he remembered his vow to list all those things he now takes for granted. Turning to a fresh page he wrote:

What relationships/people do I take for granted?

Change stirred within as he reviewed Bobby's quotes. *Ego is I. Team is we.* He thought back to Jon and the trust he put in his team. Pierce knew as well that he could take it beyond business and recognize that team leadership also applied to home life. Sarah, Lila, and Max were his team, not his subjects. It became clear that providing for them in the detached way he had done thus far was negligent at best.

Pulling into the circular driveway of the grand old Del Coronado Hotel, Pierce closed his journal feeling poised to face each new day with courage and integrity. Paying the driver before maneuvering his luggage and gimpy leg toward the check-in desk, happy memories of boyhood visits to this very resort reemerged, filling him with a giddy sense of excitement. Standing as tall as the proud palm trees flanking the entrance, his pistol cocked and ready, wings spread wide, courageous and strong, Pierce felt ready to implement change.

Acting with Courage and Integrity

Chapter 5

Doing Truly Great Things

The Third Encounter

I never wanted to be famous. I only wanted to be great.

—Ray Charles

Fond memories coupled with a balmy 75-degree temper-
ature bathed Pierce in a warm glow of happiness. San
Diego truly was magnificent in mid-October. Summer had
gracefully stepped aside, allowing fall her moment to shine as
tourists faded back to their hometowns, leaving the resort
relatively vacant.

Cool ocean waters had greatly benefited Pierce's knee
injury and forehead laceration. Sure, the forehead stung
like crazy when he first dove into the frigid October surf, but
there was nothing like a good salt bath to cleanse and heal.
In the two days Pierce had spent at the beach, most of
the scab dissolved as a fresh layer of skin emerged on the
forehead, carefully shaded by a baseball cap purchased from
the resort gift store. The swelling in his knee reduced
dramatically, allowing him to surrender the splint. Jon's cane,

however, came in very handy for evening walks along the beach.

Pierce strolled on the beach one evening as waves crashed into the shore, massaging his feet with white, foamy strokes before retreating in the moonlight. As he reflected on his serendipitous meetings with Jon and Bobby, he felt incredibly lucky. The two men had imparted important life lessons, each uniquely different, yet possessing strong nuances of leadership—*great* leadership. Both had been team players and attributed their success to it. Neither operated from the ego, or "I." They enjoyed incredible success in their respective fields and, in Pierce's eyes, appeared to have attained success and balance in life as well.

The two encounters had taught Pierce that greatness was not about putting on a show for the benefit of others, but it was about following your passion and deeper spiritual intuition. What mattered most was being honest and true to one's own inner voice of wisdom or guidance, and striving to share that sense of honesty, integrity, and inner fulfillment with others.

After working through all of Sosanna's exercises, Pierce felt energized and inspired to bring change into his life. He had grown wise enough to understand that change would not magically occur overnight, and he knew that taking time to retreat and reflect, as he had in Colorado and San Diego, was essential to any form of growth. He knew it would also require patience and hard work and, knowing what lay ahead, Pierce found himself contemplating his return to Charlotte.

When he returned to his suite just after 9 PM, he decided to call Sarah the following morning and tell her he was ready

Own YOUR Success

to come home. Following a quick shower, he retrieved his journal and daily newspapers from the large oak desk in his room and made his way downstairs to the Babcock & Story Sports Bar, ready to indulge in an evening cocktail and snack.

While Pierce sat at the beautifully handcrafted mahogany bar and enjoyed an Oban and lobster wrap, an article in *USA Today* caught his eye. He wasn't a huge sports fan, and he allowed himself little downtime to enjoy such folly. However, Pierce maintained a moderate interest in basketball, college basketball in particular. Busy or not, one really could not exist in North Carolina without being, at the very least, peripherally aware of college basketball—unless, of course, one was without pulse.

Along with fall, October ushered in the beginning of the college basketball season, entertaining fans through awkward family holiday reunions and numbing winter chills, and offering an escape from—or alternative to—Monday night football. Beyond Super Bowl hullabaloo and Saint Patrick's Day parades, college basketball culminated in one shining moment of triumph for players and fans driven by passion, not yet by dollars.

Youthful spirit pulsed through the veins of college basketball. It was gloriously celebrated by those lucky enough to be part of it, and mourned by those catching a glimpse of whoever they once were and where they had come from. No other sport or league came close. Yet, at the dawn of the college basketball season, the sports section of *USA Today* dedicated a full-page spread to a *high school* basketball coach.

However, it became apparent to Pierce while reading the article that Todd Edwards was no ordinary high school coach. Now entering his fortieth year of coaching high school, he had led a Missouri team to great victories, winning a staggering and impressive 110 straight games and notching five straight state titles. Pierce adjusted his seat, gesturing to the bartender to freshen his Oban. Smoothing the sports section out on the bar in front of him, he continued to read about this incredible man.

Coach Edwards, it appeared, played for the Wizard of Westwood—legendary coach John Wooden—alongside celebrated players such as Lew Alcindor (Kareem Abdul Jabbar) during the golden years at UCLA. "Wow," Pierce thought to himself. "What the heck is this guy doing coaching high school?" He was further intrigued as he read on to discover that while Edwards had been co-captain of the UCLA team, he was essentially a bench warmer. A quote from Wooden, prior to Edward's 2010 death, summed it up: "Edwards displayed more heart than any other player I met. On the court or off, he gave his best every day. Edwards had heart. Inspiring teammates, his spirit and energy was the very foundation of the UCLA dynasty years."

If the man known as the best coach in college basketball history saw something special in this guy, Pierce knew there had to be something to it. But why was Edwards turning down mega-offers to coach NBA and college teams? According to the article, he had consistently fielded offers throughout his 40-year career coaching high school. Even now, creeping toward 65 years of age, when he should be playing golf, he continued to field six- and seven-figure

78

Own YOUR Success

offers, yet he remained dedicated to the high school team in St. Louis that affectionately referred to him as "Coach E." He had sacrificed money, fame, and glory; he was either insane or on the verge of sainthood. Either way, Pierce was curious. By the time he finished reading the article, he knew he had to meet Coach Edwards. This was the kind of leader he needed to learn from. Building on lessons learned from Jon and Bobby, Coach E's secret strategy for winning could very well be what would set Blackbird Tech apart from the rest. Besides, St. Louis was on the way to Charlotte—kind of.

"Another great leader," Pierce thought to himself as he made his way back upstairs to his suite. A pattern appeared to be forming as the people he needed to meet manifested. Having gained so much already from other people's experiences, he acknowledged how amazing—and beneficial—it was to turn down the noise in his own head and open his mind to what others had to offer. Foolish pride had always dominated, leading him to believe he had to find all of the answers and solutions on his own. Was this unnecessary independence or blatant ignorance? Humbled by the likes of Jon, Bobby, and now Coach E, Pierce welcomed the growth rousing within. He had come so far.

■ ■ ■

"Daddy?" Lila's sweet voice came down the other end of the line.

"Hi, Sweetheart!" The crack in his voice surprised him, making him aware all at once of the deep, aching longing to see his family.

Doing Truly Great Things

"Daddy? Will you be home for Halloween?"

"Yes, Sweetheart. I would not miss that for anything."

"Mommy said I could be a princess again, like last year. And Max—Max wants to be *you* for Halloween!" She squealed with delight.

"That's a very scary costume indeed." Pierce laughed along with her, masking his tears. Max wanted to be him. "Thank goodness for this journey," Pierce thought, grateful that he was developing into a more positive role model for his young son.

"Maybe we'll alter one of your old suits for him." Sarah's voice cutting in on the line knocked the wind out of him. How he missed her.

"Hello?"

"I—I'm here." Pierce swallowed hard, choking on his tears.

"Soooo? How is sunny San Diego?"

"Beautiful. Just beautiful. I met another extraordinary person, before I even got here—on the flight! It's pretty astonishing, what people have to offer when you're willing to listen," Pierce conceded.

"Isn't it?"

"Sarah?"

"Yes?"

"Was I . . . was I really such a pompous jerk?"

Sarah laughed. "No!"

"Really? I'm beginning to get the impression I was."

"No, honey. You were just . . . closed. Cut off. To *every-thing*. Unavailable, I guess, is the word I am looking for."

"I'm sorry."

"Pierce, look at what you're doing now for us, for *yourself!* It may have taken a busted knee and snowstorm to finally capture your attention, but I guess what I am trying to say is it takes great courage to look deep inside yourself and examine what needs to change. I'm really proud of you."

Pierce remained quiet. He knew the floodgates would come crashing open if he dared speak.

"Honey?"

"I'm here," he finally mustered with a sigh. "I really miss you guys."

"We miss you too."

"I thought I was ready to come home last night—and I am, if you guys need me. I do feel ready, but—well, I was hoping to make just one last stop before I do. In St. Louis."

"St. Louis?"

"It's a long story. I'll fill you in when I come home. But I think I've found another person who I stand to learn a lot from, personally and professionally. I'm hoping he'll allow me the opportunity to pick his brain a little."

"When will you be there?"

"Tonight. If I get ahold of him and meet tomorrow, I can be home by tomorrow night!"

"Wonderful. But, Pierce, please don't feel rushed."

"I know, I know! Don't come home until I feel ready. But I am ready, Sarah. I really am. This one guy, however, appears to be a pretty inspirational individual. Given I am already on the road, I figured it would make sense to seize this opportunity and meet him."

"I'm really looking forward to hearing more about these people and experiences. Soon."

Doing Truly Great Things

"I'll call you from St. Louis."

"Love you."

"Love you too. Bye."

Replacing the phone it its cradle, Pierce stared at it for a long time. He had one more call to make. He'd taken a bit of a gamble last night and had already booked the 10 AM American Airlines flight to St. Louis with a layover in Chicago. If he could not get ahold of Coach E, he'd deplane in Chicago, shop for gifts for Sarah and the kids along the Magnificent Mile, and catch a flight home, surprising his family later that night.

Reaching for the notebook where he scribbled the number of the high school made famous by Coach E, Pierce hesitated briefly, wondering what approach to take. What would he say when—*if*—he finally got Coach E on the line? He punched the numbers in and asked the switchboard to connect him to the coach's office, figuring he would rehearse his spiel with the assistant before speaking with the coach himself.

"Coach's office." A gravelly voice picked up after only two rings, startling Pierce.

"Err . . . Coach Edwards, please."

"You got 'im."

Pierce was stunned! How was it possible that a legend—a *winner*—like Coach E would answer his own phone? Transported in time to his Charlotte office, Pierce recalled—with a touch of guilt and humiliation—his stubborn refusal to answer his own phone. He feared he would not appear important enough if he answered himself, so he ignored calls, never listening, ordering people around, and playing the role of the all-important CEO. Bobby's voice echoed in his mind: *Ego is I. Team is we.*

"Hello?" Coach E shook Pierce back to the present moment.

"Hello, Coach. I'm not quite sure how to say this, so please forgive me. My name is Pierce Edwards. I'm the CEO of Blackbird Technologies, which has absolutely nothing to do with basketball."

"God, stop rambling," Pierce chastised himself. Drawing in a deep, centering breath, he pressed on.

"Coach, I'm calling in reference to the article in yesterday's *USA Today*. First of all, I'd like to congratulate you on such a successful run. I was—*I am*—incredibly inspired by the article. I know this is going to sound a little odd, but I plan to be in St. Louis on business tomorrow, and I was wondering if I could buy you a coffee or—"

"You a journalist?"

"No, no. Pierce Edwards, same spelling as you, CEO of Blackbird Tech. We supply flight technology to the commercial and defense aero industries, a far cry from journalism! Feel free to Google me if you like. I promise not to take too much of your time; I understand you are a very busy man. . . ." He trailed off in hopeful anticipation.

"Plenty of journalists been callin' since that article went to press."

"I'm sure you've been inundated with calls."

"Inundated?" Coach scoffed. "Damn phone's been ringin' off the hook."

Once again, Pierce was blown away. One of the most successful coaches in America, who probably spent half his

Doing Truly Great Things

time fielding calls from NBA and college head hunters—and now, journalists and random strangers on soul-searching missions—had been humble enough to answer his own phone. Mentally noting yet another facet of his own behavior that needed changing, Pierce asked himself, "Why am I not like that? What made me so self-important?"

"Yours . . . Pierce, is it?"

"Yes."

"Yours is the oddest call I've received in quite a while. All day yesterday and this mornin' I've been invited to speak here, interview there, deliver graduation speeches all over the country. If I lived for 300 years I couldn't manage all of those engagements. But you, you're the only one who has asked to come to *me* . . . and you say you want to buy me a coffee?"

"Yes, sir." Pierce nervously waited for his hopes to be confirmed.

"Okay, Pierce. Every mornin' I eat breakfast at Sportsman's Park, a little hole-in-the-wall near my house that serves the best eggs in St. Louis. I'm there 7:45 AM each day. If you're in town on business, you are welcome to join me for breakfast there tomorrow."

"Yes, sir. Thank you."

"And, if you're lyin' to me and you are a journalist, I'm walkin' out."

"No. Thank you, Coach. I look forward to meeting you."

"You need the address?"

"No, thank you. I'll look it up. See you then, 7:45 AM."

Invigorated, Pierce gathered up his belongings and headed to the airport, excited about his detour to St. Louis.

■ ■ ■

As the flight began its descent over downtown St. Louis, the arch, proudly gleaming on the west bank of the Mississippi, came into view. Pierce, who had only seen the famous landmark in photographs, was impressed by its enormity. A modern piece of sculpture, it towered over the office buildings and hotels of a city often voted most dangerous in America. The iconic arch appeared to welcome visitors, proffering the possibility of duality with a sly wink. Perhaps, thought Pierce, St. Louis was telling him that this city had more to offer than what met the eye—if one took the time to look.

Even more impressive, however, was the sky—a sheet of silk dipped in vats of pastel dyes, with strips of pink, mauve, and azure stacked like a delicious layer cake. Pierce never imagined a sunset arranging such a beautiful display of color this far from the coast. The majestic show served as a gentle reminder for Pierce to let go of expectations. As the plane touched down on the runway, he vowed to do just that.

■ ■ ■

Arriving the Sportsman's Park restaurant the following morning, eager and early, Pierce kept one keen eye trained on the door as he sat in a booth sipping coffee. What felt like an eternity passed before Coach E finally crossed the threshold, the door creaking loudly in his grip. Glancing at the clock above the bar, Pierce noticed it was exactly 7:45 AM.

Recognizing him from the newspaper, Pierce excitedly raised his hand, waving the coach over to where he sat. Despite his reputation as a bench warmer, the coach was tall

85

Doing Truly Great Things

and extremely fit; it was evident the coach could still lace them up if he wanted to. In fact, he most likely played half court with buddies on a regular basis. As he strode across the dimly lit restaurant, Pierce surmised he could probably manage full court without thinking too much about it. Yet another common denominator shared by Jon, Bobby and Coach—*fitness*. Bobby, of course, was an exception, an anomaly. But Jon was 63 years old, Coach was pushing 65— and both men would run circles around Pierce when it came to fitness levels. He vowed to start running with Josh again when he got home, once his knee fully recovered. Pierce smiled as the 65-year-old man who shamed him approached the booth.

"You must be Pierce. No, don't get up." He leaned across the table, gripping Pierce's hand in a strong, firm handshake, callused from years of handling a basketball. Taking possession of the bench opposite Pierce, Coach gestured to the waitress to bring more coffee.

"Coffee here is so-so," the Coach said once the waitress was out of earshot. "I come here for the eggs." He smiled broadly, holding the mug in both hands, enjoying the warmth. Pierce was immediately reminded of Jon's habit.

"Thank you, Coach, for meeting me. I feel honored."

The coach flapped a leathery hand toward Pierce in protest. "Listen, so long as you're not a journalist. I'm happy to share my breakfast with a visitor passin' through town."

Pierce smiled at the little white lie he had told. On the phone he had been hesitant to tell the Coach he was flying in to see him specifically. He feared he would seem like some kind of crazed stalker and scare him off.

"What business you in again?"

"Technology, flight technology," Pierce offered before asking, "What is it you have against journalists?"

"Nothin' against journalists. So long as they do their job and leave me the heck alone to do mine."

"O-kay."

"Since that article ran, everybody wants an interview. I don't have time. It's basketball season, in case none of these dimwits took the time to note. I agreed to the one article and enough's enough. What more could they possibly get out of me?"

"Well, you deserve some time in the spotlight."

"Eh. Baloney!"

Pierce smiled; he had not heard somebody use that expression in the longest time. It was telling that the man seated before him, shunning the spotlight many would be proud to bask in, had plenty of character.

"I have a confession to make," Pierce could not believe the words spilling from his own mouth. Coach cocked a bushy eyebrow at him. He swallowed hard, finding the backbone to tell the truth, "I—the—the," he sighed heavily, "the only business I have in St. Louis today is meeting you. I came here, that is, specifically for that purpose."

"And you're not a journalist." Coach E eyed him suspiciously.

Pierce shook his head sincerely. "Nope. Just an admirer—the non-creepy kind, of course." He smiled apologetically as he continued. "I'm working to make changes in my personal and professional life and I've been fortunate enough to meet some formidable leaders, like you, who have shared valuable

Doing Truly Great Things

insights with me. When I read about you, I knew I had to meet you. I guess, in all earnest, I'd just like to pick your brain a little."

"That's it?"

"Well, I do have a lot of questions, of course," Pierce laughed. "What motivates you? Who inspires you? What's your secret formula to lead and produce such stellar winning teams? What do you tell your players? I could go on."

"No." Coach raised his hand, nodding his head, indicating he got Pierce's point. Handing a menu to Pierce, he said, "Best we order some breakfast. Did I mention the eggs are excellent here?"

Calling the waitress back for more coffee, the two men placed their orders. The Coach asked for his usual and Pierce, following Edwards's recommendation, ordered a spinach frittata with side of fruit. He was dying for fries but thought better than to order them in front of such a healthy human specimen.

Coach E leaned forward. Propping his elbows on the table, he rested his chin in his hands. Sighing deeply, he began, "Pierce, I hope I don't disappoint you when I tell you I have no great secrets. I've simply been a very blessed and lucky man."

Pierce's heart sank. What had he expected, really? Coach E to walk in with a plastic folder filled with the answers to life? He felt like an idiot, selfishly springing this visit on the coach. Reminding himself of his vow to let go of expectations, he refocused on what the coach was saying.

"Very blessed," Coach E went on, "blessed to have Wooden in my life. Have you read his biography?"

"Ah, no sir."

"Hmm," Coach E nodded, "Buy it . . . download it . . . whatever the heck it is you do to read a book these days. You want inspiration? I guarantee you'll find it there."

"Would you say your coaching style was influenced by Wooden?"

"My coachin' style?" Coach E's brown eyes widened, "My entire *life* was influenced by Wooden! Coach Wooden was my coach, yes. But that man did not stop coachin' when a player stepped off the court. In fact, that's when the serious coachin' began."

Pierce was glued to his seat. Whether or not he gained what he was seeking from this conversation, he was hearing first-hand stories about the greatest coach in college basketball history.

"Wooden taught me to be a great leader, as a coach, a father, *and* a human being. Surely you've heard of Wooden's *Gift of a Lifetime*? No? It's famous! Here, pass me one of those napkins." Pierce obliged, passing several flimsy paper napkins across the table.

"There are many Wooden-isms out there, but this one, *this one*, is gold," Coach E enthused as he scrawled the following on the napkin:

1. Be true to yourself.

2. Help others.

3. Make each day your masterpiece.

4. Drink deeply from good books, especially the Bible.

5. Make friendship a fine art.

Doing Truly Great Things

6. Build a shelter against a rainy day.

7. Pray for guidance and count and give thanks for your blessings every day.

Once complete, he pushed the napkin across the table to Pierce. "Treasure it."

Pierce opened and read it once before folding and placing it safely in his breast pocket.

"Is our style the same? Technically, no, we are very different. Ethically, we're similar. Wooden cared deeply about his players, on and off the court. And so do I. Developin' their ability to move forward in life as well-rounded human beings, givin' their very best each and every day is most important to me. Not as ball players, but as people. *Great people.* Those kids will always come first. They are more important to me than any damn six-figure deal—always will be. You got to be willin' to put other people in front of you. *That* I learned from Wooden."

Pierce thought about Sarah and the sacrifice she had made to help him be better, sending him off indefinitely and holding down the fort at home. He would not let her down.

"Do you pass Wooden's *Gift of a Lifetime* on to all of your players?"

"Here is what I tell my players: Go do great things. And they know I don't mean playin' ball! I expect them to give their best in each and every little thing they do. Everybody is capable of that. GDGT—they taught me the texting version! That little mantra has carried on through generations of alumni, and it continues to spread. People who don't even know me on the other side of the planet use it. Not because they saw it in an article, but because they heard it from a friend of a friend of a former player of mine who is out there livin' it. Every day."

"So you created a legacy, just like Wooden's *Gift*." Pierce tapped the pocket holding the napkin.

"Wooden was a great storyteller. I'm no storyteller. God, that man could tell a story! You really should get that book." Coach E clapped his hands together as the waitress arrived at the table. "Ah! What did I tell you? Here we go—best eggs in St. Louis."

Pierce's stomach growled at the sight of the food; he was starving. "Your team has consistently achieved some pretty great things on the court too, you know."

Coach E raised his hand. "Ech! We don't talk about winnin' or losin'. It doesn't matter! The *process* is what matters. Not the results, but how you *get* there."

"Are you seriously telling me you don't care about winning?"

"It doesn't matter what happens once you're there. If you have not been passionate and focused on the journey, it was a complete waste of time. Pointless." He dug in to his food. "Aren't these eggs great?"

"But how can you not be thinking about results if that's what you are ultimately working toward?"

Coach put his fork down. "Pierce, you work toward *goals*. Results are an expectation, of which we have little control over the outcome." Pierce smiled, enjoying a twilight zone moment, as he considered the vow he made touching down in St. Louis.

"Pierce, you came to me for guidance. You told me you wanted to implement changes and that you believed I could help you."

Pierce nodded, taking a bite of his frittata.

"Did you come here with a certain expectation of the outcome of this meeting? Knowing what I would—or should—tell you?"

Pierce was not sure what to say. Admittedly, he had arrived with expectations of learning something from the coach. Given his success, how could he not have knowledge or precious pearls of wisdom to share?

"Life is challengin'. Financial markets swing wildly, pressures come at us from every angle—work, friends, and family—and obstacles stand in our way. Sometimes that is all we can see, as we clutch desperately to what we want, what we *think* should happen. External obstructions standin' in the way, or creatin' distraction, only add to our anxiety, and, ultimately, feelings of failure and inadequacy. But what if each day could be a small victory?" He paused. Rapping his knuckles against the table, emphasizing each word, he added, "You-slowly-inch-toward-success."

"Coach E, forgive me, but I've always been very result driven; so I'm having trouble wrapping my head around this. What makes a day—or anything, for that matter—victorious if you're not focused on some kind of result?"

"By focusin' on daily activities and small goals, you can develop a passion for the *process*. And this kind of passion gives you the opportunity to make every single day triumphant." Coach tapped the table with his knuckles once again for emphasis. "Success follows naturally, *organically*, without tryin' to control the outcome. This is what I call my *Prize-fighter Day* method." The coach paused; noticing Pierce's confused expression, he checked his watch before adding, "I need to be at school just after nine. Pass me those napkins again."

This time Pierce passed the whole aluminum napkin holder across the table. Pinching one from the top of the pile, coach spread it out on the table. Writing the words *YOUR PRIZEFIGHTER DAY* along the top of the thin napkin, he underlined them and looked to Pierce. "Identify three activity-driven things that will leave you feelin' victorious if you accomplish them today."

The question took Pierce by surprise. "I—I don't know."

"Look, for simplicity's sake, we'll do one personal, one business, and one that is about helpin' somebody else." He wrote the numbers 1, 2, and 3 on the far left side of the napkin, allowing space between each to write the answers.

"Okay." Pierce felt a cocktail of skepticism and uncertainty stirring within.

Observing Pierce's face, Coach joked, "If you learn somethin' you'll really feel victorious, huh? Let's look at one. *Personal.*" He wrote the word on the napkin. "Wakin' up an hour earlier to get your workout in would be a personal, activity-driven accomplishment. You feel good from the endorphins, which gives you the confidence to go out and do great things."

Next to the number two, Coach wrote the word *Professional.* "A business-related activity could be, in a sales career for example, setting a goal to make a specific number of

Doing Truly Great Things

calls—regardless of the results. Remember, we are focused on the calls, the *process*."

Finally, next to number three, Coach wrote *Helping Others*. "To be of service to another. Now this is what life is about. We are all in this together, and we are all here to help one another. To make and accomplish one, just one goal, to reach out to somebody—without personal or professional gain in mind—you are on the path to true greatness. It can be a phone call to somebody close to you, a colleague, or somebody in need, or simply pickin' up the neighbor's kids from school."

"You do this every day?"

"Every day. Create three *activity-driven* focal points—you understand? Meanin' you have to get off your butt and take action. This will give you the sense of accomplishment necessary to create personal and professional balance in life. Once you make this simple exercise a habit, you will imperceptibly pull away from old, disempowerin' patterns. Even the most ordinary of days will become *your* Prizefighter Day."

"What if you don't accomplish one or two things on your list?"

"Pierce, you would only fail to accomplish somethin' if you were focused on the outcome. You'll always complete an activity that you know fires you up and ignites your passion—and you will do well. The only thing that may go wrong, so to speak, is it may not result in the outcome you expected. Once you let go of that, you have accomplishment. You have passion. You will go do great things. Every day."

Pierce soaked it in. He understood the coach's method in theory, but shifting his focus from results to activities would require a lot of mental retraining. It was, essentially, a totally different blueprint on how to live. He hoped he could do it. The resistance he felt within only affirmed that it was, most likely, *exactly* what he needed to do in order to facilitate real change.

"Pierce, it was nice meetin' you. Before I leave, I also have a confession."

Pierce looked up, surprised.

"Like you, I once tracked down a woman, a doctor, following an interview she did with CNN. I'm not sure how much time you have, but if you really want to be in the presence of true greatness, I recommend you visit Dr. Rose Barnes, in Boston. I shape lives; but Dr. Barnes has dedicated hers to savin' them. She epitomizes what it means to do truly great things. She's creatin' a legacy."

"Coach, I can't thank you enough." Pierce shook his hand. "And I must tell you, what you do for these kids, your dedication to them and sacrifice to coach them, turning away from money and fame—it is extremely noble."

"You are correct, Pierce; it *is* noble. But I don't do it for nobility. I do it because it's my passion. It is where my heart is." He patted Pierce on the shoulder and headed for the exit. The Wooden quote came to mind: *Edwards had heart.* Yes, Pierce thought, he sure does.

Stopping short of the door, the coach turned to him one last time. "Rose Barnes," he called across the restaurant, "Dr. Rose Barnes." Then he was gone.

Doing Truly Great Things

Sitting in the booth, Pierce spread the napkins out in front of him. He tried to focus, but all he could hear was Coach's voice: *She is creating a legacy*. What did that really mean? He loved the word, loved the concept of legacy, but what did it actually mean to be creating one? Wasn't that result driven?

Not if she is focusing solely on her work and her fight to help others. The legacy is simply being created as a direct result of her dedication. Now he understood. Coach E had introduced him to an entirely different viewpoint. And like Jon, Coach E had shared his secret, but Pierce was the one who would have to do the work.

A fire in his belly ignited, burning with excitement at the possibility of another encounter. Exhausted, Pierce pushed it aside. Gathering up the napkins, he folded them carefully and placed them in his pocket before asking for the check.

He noticed that the waitress was tied up on a phone order, and pulled his BlackBerry out. It felt foreign without personalization, and he could not wait to get home and synch it with his PC so he could load his photos back on it. He longed to see his family and he did not have a single picture of them. Only the one etched in his mind, now blurred at the edges because he had been gone so long. Memory was a funny—and often cruel—thing.

Pierce typed "Rose Barnes MD" into the search engine. Almost immediately, pages of results flashed on the screen, which was one advantage to not having his "stuff" loaded on the BlackBerry—speed. Sighing heavily, he pushed it aside. Was he really thinking about making one more stop? Who would he be putting first if he did—himself, Sarah and the kids, or the company? Realizing the answer was all three, he tried an alternate method of reasoning. Would meeting Dr. Barnes help him personally, professionally, or inspire him to help others? Once again, the answer was all three.

Reluctantly, he called Sarah.

"Hey. It's me."

"What's wrong? Is everything okay? Are you still in St. Louis?"

"I'm great, and in St. Louis . . . still."

"Honey, you sound terrible. Are you sure you're okay?"

"Yeah, I am. The coach, the guy I came to see, he really made me think. To the point that I am quite literally recalibrating my mind. It's exhausting!"

"Well, that's good . . . I think."

"No, it's *really* good. He introduced me to unique way of looking at things. It was definitely worth the stop."

"So?"

"Well, I really do want to come home . . . but . . . ."

"Pierce, honey? If you need to stay away longer, or make another stop, that's fine. We miss you terribly, but you've got to do what you feel is right in order to complete this journey of self-exploration."

"Boston. I'm stopping in Boston and then I—" He stopped short of making a promise he could not be certain of keeping. "Well, we'll see."

"Yes, we will. Love you. Travel safe!"

"I will. Love you more. Bye."

Pierce called American Airlines from the rental car. Luckily there was an 11 AM flight to Boston routing, once again, through Chicago. Placing the napkins safely in his journal, the Douglas International logo on the price tag caught his eye. He ran his hand over the sturdy black cover, recalling all that had happened since he purchased the book. So much wisdom held within a simple $4.95 notebook. He wondered what more lay ahead.

Chapter 6

Creating a Living Legacy

The Fourth Encounter

It's not how long you live. It's how you choose to live your life.

—Janet Fishman Newman

St. Louis's Lambert International Airport had undergone major restoration since the 2011 Good Friday tornado. As he made his way through the American Airlines terminal, Pierce wondered whether renovations to the new and contemporary wing had been under way when the tornado hit, or if Mother Nature's fury had provided the catalyst for change. It seemed to him that transformation occurred consciously as part of one's natural evolution. If not, catastrophe stepped in, walloping one across the back of the head, creating the seismic shift that made it necessary to facilitate change.

He checked his messages one last time as he boarded the flight to Boston. Nothing. Two hours ago he had called Dr. Barnes's office at the Amyloidosis Research Center she headed at Boston Medical Center. The curt yet amiable receptionist had assured Pierce that Dr. Barnes's schedule was booked. The busy doctor had no available appointments for up to three weeks. When using charm failed, Pierce frankly and honestly explained the reason that he wanted to meet with Dr. Barnes, and promised not to take too much of her time. Understanding that her patients were an absolute priority, he even offered to accept an appointment on standby terms. The receptionist took his number and agreed to see what she could do to squeeze him in. He really hoped he was not making the trip to Boston in vain.

Coach Edwards had planted the seed of intrigue, and the online research Pierce conducted in the club lounge fertilized and nurtured it. Dr. Rose Barnes, internationally recognized in her field, was a powerhouse. She was revolutionizing treatments that allowed patients suffering from this rare, deadly disease to live. At the age of 74, she was someone who had literally dedicated her life to finding a cure for this disease, and she remained unstoppable. Whether or not she could truly demonstrate the answer to the riddle Coach Edwards had surreptitiously presented to Pierce—how to create a legacy without being result driven—did not matter. Pierce simply wanted to enjoy a moment in the presence of yet another inspirational hero.

He closed his eyes as he settled into his seat, pondering exactly what the term "legacy" meant to him. Wasn't it what we all wanted: the opportunity to leave an impression here on earth? Procreating did not seem to be enough. Only two or three generations—sometimes less—passed before you were forgotten, or at the very least, faded to a distant, irrelevant memory. Did the desire to leave this kind of a mark come from vanity? Did people create it consciously, or did it come as a direct result of single-minded conscientiousness or passion for a cause? Pierce's conversation with Coach Edwards led him to believe that it was the latter. But how could one work toward leaving one's mark on the world without being result driven? The more he thought about it, the more confused and tired he became. He gently closed his eyes to meditate and clear his thoughts, and slipped off instead into a light slumber.

The plane touched down in Boston just after 5 o'clock in the evening, and Pierce enjoyed the cool October air caressing his face as he made his way to the cab stand. After retrieving the messages on his voicemail, he was thrilled to learn Dr. Barnes would see him the following day at 11 AM. Pierce looked forward to a quiet evening, perhaps some good seafood—and most definitely an early night.

■ ■ ■

Pierce arrived early for his appointment and sat on the comfortable sofa provided in the open waiting area. A large glass atrium filled the reception area with natural sunlight. To the left of the reception desk sat a shiny, black grand piano begging to be played while, just behind Pierce, the filter pump for a massive tropical fish tank gurgled its own symphony. Nature's gifts had been carefully prescribed to ease the nerves of waiting patients and their loved ones.

Dr. Barnes's receptionist was less curt and much more amiable in person. "You would be surprised how many people call to meet with Dr. Barnes for reasons similar to yours." She smiled at Pierce, placing a large glass of water on the marble table beside him. "She's a very inspiring woman."

Creating a Living Legacy

"Thank you. For the water, and for squeezing me in."

"Oh, no problem. She loves meeting and helping people. Right now happens to be a very busy time; we're hosting two global conferences and Dr. Barnes is a key speaker at both, along with current clinical studies and patients . . . well, you get the picture. Lucky for you she is a huge fan of Coach Edwards."

Pierce was visibly startled by the reference to Coach E.

Reading his expression, she added, "They're old friends. He called her directly not long after you called me. She's the one who squeezed you in; I had little to do with it." Watching her walk back to her desk, Pierce remained speechless. Coach E called and got him in. How could he have been so certain Pierce would come to Boston? Laughing to himself, he realized Coach E was smart enough to know there was no way he would *not*.

Touching the cane propped up next to him—Jon's cane, or Sosanna's—Pierce felt humbled by all of the wisdom to which he had been exposed over the past couple of weeks. It was hard to believe he had gotten as far in life as he had without the help of these people, who all seemed to know and understand him so well.

"Pierce?"

He glanced up.

"Dr. Barnes is ready for you, if you'd like to follow me."

Pierce rose and followed her out of the open waiting area, past a small, private inpatient waiting room, and down a long corridor. As they made their way farther along, he noted the corridor's gray linoleum flooring was heavily worn and cracked. The receptionist showed him in to the last door at the end of the passage and offered another glass of water before leaving. The windowless office was nothing more than an eight-by-eight cell. Harsh overhead fluorescent lighting flickered above the sturdy wooden desk, laden with piles of patient files. Pierce lowered himself into a worn vinyl chair, taking in the battered and dented floor-to-ceiling metal filing cabinets surrounding him. A stark contrast to the sleek reception area, it was evident that this department of Boston Medical severely lacked financial backing.

"Pierce, welcome." Dr. Barnes entered briskly, shaking his hand before taking her seat behind the desk.

"Dr. Barnes, thank you so much for taking the time to meet with me." Pierce worked hard to contain his surprise. Dr. Barnes was a warrior by virtue and credentials, but in person, standing at barely five-feet-two, Rose Barnes was diminutive! *She has to weigh 80 pounds soaking wet!* Pierce thought to himself.

Dr. Barnes's dark olive skin fell into deep folds, rippling across her small, round face, framed by a short crop of tightly wound, snow-white curls. Leaning on her desk, she smiled at Pierce, her warm brown eyes sparkling with vitality. The hands of time had undeniably staked their claim, etching their marks on her face and body, but her vibrancy and passion for life had the last laugh, echoing heartily from deep within, far out of their reach.

"And how is my good friend Todd?" she asked, slightly amused.

"Coach E? He's great."

She smiled affectionately. "Any friend of Coach E is a friend of mine. I am sorry I do not have time to take you to lunch while you are visiting; we're in the midst of hosting two conferences and I am tied up with speaking engagements all afternoon. So, please forgive me, Pierce, if I appear rushed; but let me ask: What exactly can I help you with today?"

"Dr. Barnes, please, no need to apologize. Thank you again for making some time in your schedule for me." He sighed, gathering his thoughts to best summarize the reason for his visit. "Coach E had wonderful things to say about you and, well—he suggested you may be the person who could help me define legacy—or at the very least inspire me to explore what imprint I might leave."

"He did?" She laughed, shaking her head in mock disbelief. Sighing dramatically, she added, "Oh, Coach E."

Clasping her tiny hands in a firm grip, she locked them beneath her chin, rested them there, and thought for a moment before beginning.

"Coach E and I first met over 20 years ago. I had finally achieved a major breakthrough in a clinical trial, and CNN vetted me with a feature interview. To be honest, I only agreed to the interview in the hope of bringing some awareness"— she gestured around her—"and *funding* to our department. Following that interview, Coach E was one of many who tracked me down to congratulate me. He also had an unusual request: He wanted me to speak to some of his students. I had spoken to many a confused college grad by that point in my career, and made multiple graduation speeches. I still do. But what intrigued me back then was that he wanted me to talk to *high school* kids and try to inspire them before they even got to college. Now *that* was something new for me." She smiled at Pierce. "I've been talking to younger kids and prior students of Todd's ever since. I get very excited about the opportunity to meet new people and share my perspective and experiences. After all, we are always learning—right?"

"I hope so." He smiled expectantly at her.

"My life's work and passion has been—still *is*—amyloid research. I'm living it. I see the fruits of my labor daily, witnessing the lives I touch and the difference I make now. Of course, my hope is that the work I've started will continue once I am gone, through other doctors and future breakthroughs. And I guess you would call this legacy."

"So, you never consciously set out to create a legacy for yourself?"

Dr. Rose Barnes's face erupted in delighted laughter. "No! Well, not legacy in the terms I believe you are thinking. However, I did intend to create and focus on a *living* legacy. Something I felt would bring purpose, passion, and meaning into my life. The rest—the accolades, the imprint, as you called it—follow naturally."

"Coach E's method is to focus on the journey, and *not* the result. Do you believe this fits with consciously creating a legacy?"

"Yes. Yes, I do. You don't need to focus on the result. Your job is to define your passion and create your living legacy with a commitment to leadership and excellence, and to serving others. Do great things *now* in your life. See the lives you impact firsthand. So what if someone honors you when you are dead? What good is that?"

"So what exactly is a *living* legacy?"

Dr. Barnes paused for a moment, gathering her thoughts. "What it means to me, Pierce, is surrendering to a greater

105

Creating a Living Legacy

purpose than myself. It's not just about living my legacy today but establishing lessons to leave behind so others can learn from my experiences—good and bad. Individuals can learn from the great mentors who impacted *my* life. I am more than happy to pass their wisdom on, too."

"What's driven you to stick with this all of these years," he gestured around him, "through lack of funding, and, not to be rude, but beyond your retirement years? What drives you to keep going?"

"My patients and their families and the loved ones they may leave behind."

Selecting a patient folder from a pile on her desk, she held it up for Pierce to see. "See this, how old and tattered and worn it is?"

He nodded encouragingly, curious where she is going with this.

"Only recently did I get a visit from this patient's daughter. She's grown now, has children of her own—a beautiful, beautiful woman. Her mother passed away more than two decades ago. She discovered an old journal kept during her treatment, and had read about her mother's time here at BM. She was a young child when she lost her mother, largely kept in the dark about the disease that stole her away. As an adult and young mother herself, she felt inclined to do her own research to gain closure and understanding. The discovery of the journal led her to me." Dr. Barnes placed the file back on her desk with extreme care, delicately, as though the file itself were a fragilely ill patient.

"To give you a little background, primary amyloidosis descends on an individual without warning. The symptoms are vague, usually interpreted as hypochondria or 'nonsense,' or misdiagnosed as a less-serious disorder. They affect the major organ systems with life-threatening consequences, and there's never been a specific medicine or course of treatment for amyloidosis. Doctors were limited to prescribing treatments that would slow disease progression or treat the presenting condition rather than amyloidosis itself.

"Yet over time, my team and I here have worked with countless patients on countless studies to discover that high-dose chemotherapy treatments could help some patients live with primary amyloidosis. Far from a cure, of course; but it was a life-extending discovery for many patients. Unfortunately, it came a little too late for this particular patient. But without her, we may never have discovered this break-through. Hers was one of the main cases and courses of treatment that led to this discovery." Pierce watched as Dr. Barnes wrestled the emotion rising in her voice. Gently closing her eyes, she composed herself with several long, deep, controlled breaths.

Observing Dr. Barnes, Pierce was immediately reminded of Jon and Bobby. Her use of breathing work to center herself when emotions caught her off guard paralleled Jon's center-ing techniques. Bobby would have admired her humility— her tendency to credit her team and not herself for the life-changing treatments discovered under her leadership. It appeared that the highly successful people Pierce had encountered shared very similar habits and inner wisdom.

"Can you imagine how it felt telling this young woman, that while fatal, her mother's battle with this disease resulted in changing its course for patients diagnosed after her?

107

Creating a Living Legacy

Bittersweet. Her mother's death ultimately saved or extended many other lives." Her eyes met Pierce's directly. "Now *that's* legacy."

"Do you still hope to find a cure?"

"Of course! I plan on fighting this to the end, Pierce. I'm not just speaking for patients and their families, but for the medical community too. It's as much about the caregivers to me as it is the patients."

Pierce gave her a surprised look.

"Trauma stewardship breeds a very real problem. Like most people, I am sure you only think about the patient in terms of pain and suffering when it comes to serious diseases like amyloidosis. And it's true that working with these patients, and finding a cure for them is the very core of my work. But one must also view the big picture—the doctors, nurses, caregivers and volunteers who work with these patients all suffer greatly too. Going from room to room, from patient to patient, takes a cumulative toll on medical providers and caregivers, mentally and emotionally. Walking a couple of floors within this research hospital alone you will see patient after patient, suffering immensely, their eyes filled with hope. Most are putting every last ounce of hope they can muster in experimental treatments. As a medical provider, it is very challenging to remain unaffected by their pain."

Patting a pile of patient folders for emphasis, she reiterated, "My patients have always been my primary inspiration, but this big-picture thinking is also what drove me to never give up. A patient can receive morphine to ease his or her pain. The medical provider . . . the family . . . well, you get the idea."

Pierce nodded. "I never thought about it that way."

"Not many people do. Look at your own company, Pierce. Do you ever think about the hardships that individuals may be experiencing in their lives while they work for you? Or do you think only in terms of your profit and success?"

Pierce's face flushed red with shame.

"I don't mean to judge, Pierce; I'm merely giving an example of how reframing your thinking can help you to better understand the enormity of certain situations and the peripheral effects. The ripple of a single event in one's life can make either a positive or negative impact that can be felt far and wide. We rarely stop to question what someone's pain may actually reflect, or how deep it runs—beyond the patient, beyond the daily grind of an employee's workday. There is always a bigger picture, beyond you or what you see."

Reaching for a framed black-and-white photograph on her desk, she handed it to Pierce. "My maternal grandfather, Grossvater Mertz. Toward the end of 1937, my mother and grandmother escaped Nazi Germany. She was just 25 years old. My grandfather planned to join them soon after, but . . . well, nobody knows for certain what happened to him, but we can make an educated guess, no? Grossvater Mertz was the local shoemaker in my mother's small village. He was highly skilled and cunning, and fashioned special hollow-soled shoes that could be stuffed with gold coins so my family would have money when they arrived in the United States.

"On the journey here my mother met and befriended the man who later would become my father. I was born a little over a year after they arrived. We all lived together in a small

Creating a Living Legacy

apartment, scared, unwanted refugees learning how to survive in a strange land. We were poor, but if not for Grandfather, we would have had absolutely nothing. I was an American, having been born here—but that did not buy the family any favors. Life was incredibly hard for all of us, particularly in those early years." Dr. Barnes extended her hand to Pierce as she took the photograph back. Holding it in both hands she stared into her grandfather's eyes for a long moment before replacing it on her desk.

"As I grew up and began my education, receiving scholarships along the way, I appreciated what many of my peers took for granted. The sacrifice I needed to make in order to study and work hard paled in comparison to the great sacrifices my family had made, the *risks* they had taken. Grossvater Mertz has never been far from our family; we relive his memory and the story of how he got us here at all of our gatherings. Even as a very young girl, I had a profound understanding that each opportunity coming my way was due to him and the sacrifices and choices he made. I owed it to him to work hard at school, to honor humanity, to leave a legacy of my own, if you will. My legacy is his; it is something I honestly cannot claim for myself." She paused for a moment, her own epiphany catching her off guard.

"Pierce, people do not seek hardship in their lives. Nobody asks for a disease to ravage their body. Nobody wants to be crippled by poverty, or chased from their homeland like animals . . ." She trailed off. "I guess what I am trying to say, Pierce, is that if we possess the ability like my grandfather's to make a difference or to be of service to others, then it is our duty to do so."

She nodded toward the photograph. "Do you think he wondered what his legacy would be? No; he was merely thinking about his family's survival." She tapped the patient's folder with her knuckle. "Do you think *she* was thinking about legacy? No, she was focused on survival too. Yes, for herself; but also for her young children. So they would not lose their mother. Most legacies that I witness come as a result of people selflessly committing to help and serve others, surrendering to a cause much greater than them."

"Like you."

"Perhaps." She smiled back at Pierce, humbled by the compliment. "I've always focused on the possibility of survival for my patients, and giving their families and caregivers a better quality of life. It has never been about me. The only thing I ever set out to do, beyond helping those suffering, was to honor my grandfather's great sacrifice. To pay tribute to what my family affectionately refers to as the hollow-shoe legacy." She smiled.

As the phone on her desk lit up, Pierce recognized the receptionist's voice over the intercom and he knew his time with Dr. Barnes had come to an end. The doctor gathered several files and notebooks together; he assumed they were for her afternoon's speaking engagements. He wondered if he would have her energy when he was 74. He certainly hoped so.

Tucking the notebooks and files under one arm, Rose Barnes walked around the desk to where Pierce stood, towering over her. "Before I show you out, I'd like to give you a little parting gift."

Pierce raised a quizzical eyebrow. Had this incredibly busy woman's time not been gift enough? Offering Pierce a stapled document, she said, "This is a copy of my living legacy statement. I wrote it over 30 years ago, when my first grant for amyloid research was approved." Holding the paper in her tiny hands, she continued: "Pierce, we experience two kinds of relationships in life. There are your advocates—the individuals who *believe* in you, who support you and help you grow. Your advocates are the people who, when you say it, they believe it. Then there are adversaries—individuals who don't believe in you and battle to hold you back. Simply said, they are the ones who, when you say it, they believe *against* it."

Dr. Barnes pressed her legacy statement into Pierce's grip. "Focus on the advocates and do not give voice to your adversaries. Most importantly, Pierce: Be *your own* number one advocate. Believe in yourself. Feel free to use my legacy statement as a guide to create your own. My hope is that it helps you to find and stay on your own path to success. Shall we?" Gesturing toward the door, she smiled warmly.

Together they walked in silence to the end of the long corridor. They were quite an amusing sight: the diminutive powerhouse with her giant, crippled—and *humbled*—student. Crossing the threshold into the bright and happy reception area felt like stepping through a time machine. "How unfair," Pierce thought, "that people affected by certain diseases may never find a cure due to lack of funding. And how lucky for humanity that dedicated doctors, unmotivated by money, like Dr. Barnes, exist."

Pierce broke the silence. "Thank you, Dr. Barnes." He was speaking from his heart for the hundreds, if not thousands, of lives her tireless work had impacted.

She turned, looking up at Pierce one last time. "Remember, Pierce, it is not how long you live, but how you choose to live your life. God bless you." Walking across the lobby toward the conference rooms, far from her tired, shabby office, she left him standing in the bright, shiny, new reception area.

Sinking into the same sofa where he had waited earlier that morning, Pierce read Dr. Rose Barnes's living legacy statement. She had stuck a small yellow Post-it to the top left corner, a note for Pierce in tiny, neat cursive writing.

> *Pierce,*
>
> *I hope this helps you better understand the power of vision and purpose in terms of creating a living legacy.*
>
> *God Bless,*
>
> *Rose Barnes, MD*

Pierce read the living legacy statement several times. He could hear Rose's passion in the writing as clearly as he heard it in her voice during their 30-minute meeting. *I want to have the opportunity to protect children. And to protect mothers, fathers, and families. To find the cure for amyloidosis, allowing patients to experience their own future and live out their legacies.*

Consciously aware of the power this paper held, Pierce read it again. Written more than 30 years ago, the paper showed that its author had diligently worked to make each word become the truth. And she was not through working. Dr. Barnes was *still* fighting to find a complete cure!

Creating a Living Legacy

Amyloidosis was obviously something that kept her up at night—through the discovery of life-extending therapies, to ultimately finding a cure. How had she managed to stay so clearly and precisely focused on her goals when naysayers abounded, holding back funding and support? How had she not strayed from this path?

Pierce found his answer as he read through the statement one more time. At the top of both pages was an instruction the doctor had written to herself all of those years ago. *I must commit to reading this statement every morning and every night to be certain I am always doing my best to achieve my activity goals each and every day.* Not only had she defined her legacy, but increased the probability of its playing out over time by focusing on it each and every day.

Pierce sat back, absorbing the impact this pioneering woman had made on him. He watched as another woman, about 35 years old, wheeled her mother into the reception area, and he wondered if the patient's daughter Dr. Barnes had discussed felt anger that it had taken so long to find a therapy that could have saved her mother. How unjust it must feel when a cure or treatment comes along for an illness that took a loved one away. He hoped she found peace and comfort in the fact that her sad and lonely childhood had not been in vain. Thanks to her, countless children had been spared the loss and pain she had suffered.

Retrieving his luggage from behind the reception desk, where staff had kindly stored it, Pierce took one last look round the grand waiting area of Boston Medical. Greatly inspired by Dr. Rose Barnes, Pierce felt ready to define his legacy.

Chapter 7

Pierce Returns

You can't always choose the path you walk in life, but you can always choose the manner in which you walk it.

—John O'Leary

As he eased himself into the cab's back seat, Pierce acknowledged that Rose Barnes had been the cherry on top of the proverbial ice cream. Looking back at the lessons extracted from each encounter, he applied them all to Rose Barnes, MD. Ticking them off as he went, she met each and every mark. It was now time to apply these lessons to his life.

Visualizing Jon Davis, Bobby Rehnquist, Coach Edwards, and Dr. Rose Barnes in his mind's eye, he wondered what he would take from each encounter as he moved forward. Pierce asked himself the following questions:

Do I believe in myself, and the talents I have been given, in order to make a difference?

Will I move forward truthfully, acting with courage and integrity?

Will I choose to do truly great things?

Will I create a living legacy?'

And, the most important question: *Am I willing to change?*

Pierce was well aware that the opportunity of meeting these people and seeking their advice in terms of discovering his path was only one, very small, part of the equation. It would all be meaningless unless he chose to make the necessary changes. He closed his eyes and thought hard about this. It was all very well to be caught up in the excitement of the moment, of the possibility; but the hard work it would take to identify and implement change was yet to come. After all, he had been inspired by others in the past, and repeatedly failed to execute change once the novelty wore off. How would this time be any different?

Directing his thoughts deep within to his true inspirations, Sarah, Lila and Max, Pierce knew this time would be different because it *had* to be. Pierce affirmed, with unwavering faith, that he was ready to change.

Deciding to surprise Sarah and the kids, Pierce boarded his 2:35 PM flight to Charlotte unannounced. His heart leapt with excitement at the notion of seeing his family and holding them in his arms. Eager to get home and back to his life—the new and improved version—Pierce felt ready to make a difference. He wanted more than anything to be a better husband, father, friend, and leader, at work and home.

He had met four incredible people over the course of just 11 days; two by complete chance, the other two orchestrated. Pierce spent the duration of the 90-minute flight from Boston's Logan airport reviewing the journal notes he had made following each encounter. Taking his pen to the pages one last time, he allocated each person one page, writing each name at the top in bold print. One by one, he summarized the valuable and powerful lessons shared by each individual.

Jon Davis

Attaining Belief in Yourself

Great leaders believe in others. To believe in others, one must first believe in self.

Using meditation and mindfulness to gain focus and clarity—slowing down and thinking before acting. Acting with purpose, intention, and awareness at all times.

Sosanna's method for attaining belief in self—exercise in magazine article. Review!!!

Lieutenant J. Bobby Rehnquist

Acting with Courage and Integrity

Identifying truth, and acting from there with courage and integrity.

TEAM WORK—Ego is I, Team is WE

Appreciating all people and the selfless acts and sacrifices they make daily.

The only easy day was yesterday.

Coach Todd Edwards
    Doing Truly Great Things
    Be willing to put other people in front of you. Be willing to be of service to others.
    GO DO GREAT THINGS! GDGT!!!
    Prizefighter Day—setting attainable activity goals daily, personal, business, and service. Make each day VICTORIOUS!

Dr. Rose Barnes
    Creating a Living Legacy
    Surrender to a cause greater than yourself.
    Create a living legacy and work diligently to fulfill it. Fight for what you believe in, regardless of the odds stacked up against you.

■ ■ ■

Wheeling his luggage behind him for the very last time on this journey, Pierce grinned from ear to ear as he made his way to the cab stand. It felt *great* to be back in Charlotte, North Carolina. As he turned off the interstate toward his suburban home, a massive billboard came into view.

TRUST IN THE GREATNESS OF OTHERS

Which of the four mentors arranged that, he wondered in disbelief. Why had he never seen the billboard before? Or was this yet another sign in his life he had failed to pay attention to? *Trust in the greatness of others.* To get to where he already was in life, Pierce knew he had possessed the required talent, intelligence, and leadership skills to be successful. Where he had failed was in clutching too tightly, trying to control everything. He had failed to *trust.*

Seeing that billboard drove home the incredible lessons he had learned from his four new mentors. The billboard was the exclamation point that summed up his journey. In that moment, Pierce clearly understood that leveraging more and trusting in others' abilities would enable him to make a much more significant impact in both his professional and personal lives. Once again, he asked himself some direct and pointed questions:

Who will I surround myself with?

Where will I focus my energy?

Who will be on my team, giving me the confidence and strength to act courageously and with integrity?

It was easy for Pierce to identify one of the very first changes he would implement. As of the following day, he would step down as CEO of Blackbird Tech. Anderson had more than proven his ability during Pierce's absence. Pierce planned to draw on Navy SEAL protocol and work with Anderson to deconstruct the corporate pyramid, replacing it with a strong, capable, and *equal* team. As chairman of the board, Pierce would remain peripherally involved, guiding and inspiring the team to build the company to its fullest potential. After all, he now had four

119

Pierce Returns

amazing lessons to share with those he influenced and about whom he cared greatly.

As the cab turned onto his property, Pierce's heart raced at the prospect of seeing the three people who meant the most to him. Snaking slowly down the long, winding driveway, Pierce noticed that the poplars were leading the fall parade and beginning to turn, boasting a golden-yellow hue. Smiling, he knew he had made it home in time for the grand old show at the end of the month—the neighborhood kids prowling the streets in costume, while he and Sarah enjoyed fall's fiery display with a glass of wine on the deck. It was something they had not done in the five years they had lived in this house—just one tradition of many that Pierce couldn't wait to begin observing again.

Waving the cab driver off, Pierce stood and stared at his house. *Obnoxiously large*, he thought to himself, laughing in disbelief at how much he had changed. Only 11 days earlier, he had believed this house represented the pinnacle of success. Dragging his luggage toward the rear door that led into the kitchen, he picked up as much speed as he could muster, as Jon's cane crunched in the gravel with a rhythmic thud. He was making his way to what he had finally come to understand was the true measure of his success: the three very special people inside.

Appendix
Exercises for YOUR Path to Greatness

Five Key Factors for Attaining Belief in Yourself

1. *Accept the truth:* Realizing and identifying with the person you are today is the key to becoming the person you want to be. Remember the lesson Pierce learned: We never actually *fail* in life. We just don't always get the results that we want. You cannot live a lie. You have to acknowledge and identify with what is most important in your life to ultimately attain belief in yourself.

2. *Speak the truth:* You may be reluctant—even scared— to talk about or acknowledge past behavior and habits that you regret. However, avoiding them only serves to amplify the pain and make us feel like victims. Get the truth out into the light by talking about your experiences with a trusted friend or a professional.

3. *Breathe through the truth:* Even though every fiber of your being wants to react by believing that your actions up to this point have been correct, know that you can change. Avoid acting from a place of pain or anger. The best way to reclaim your dignity is to

behave rationally and treat yourself lovingly, which will keep you from self-destructing.

4. *Process the truth:* Give yourself time and space to find your equilibrium. Believe confidently and whole-heartedly that making these changes will prompt you to develop a stronger foundation. However, recognize that this will take time, and give yourself that time.

5. *Create a plan based on the truth:* Don't expect things to be perfect right away; you can't simply flip a switch and have a new life. Old behaviors and mind-sets often come back into the realm. Stay strong and acknowledge that you must continue to believe and actively engage in this process in order to experience concrete change for your future. With this in mind, define how you want to live your life from now on.

Take out a piece of paper and write down any idea about the person you want to be and the life you want to live. Once you have clarity on this, you can take concrete steps toward realizing your goals and *Attaining Belief in Yourself.*

YOUR Prizefighter Day Exercise

The world in which we live today has become complex, constantly moving at high speed, with financial markets swinging up and down. We face professional pressures as well obstacles with friends and family along the natural ebb and flow of life. What if there was a way that you could target each and every day as a victory by focusing on daily activities, rather than trying to hold on too tightly to results that you ultimately cannot control?

The most accomplished individuals find great success when they focus on developing and exhibiting passion for the *process*. If you choose to make it so, every single day can be a victory. The following will help you achieve your *Prizefighter Day*.

> *The Key: Identify three activity-driven goals that if accomplished will make today victorious, regardless of any other obstacles that come your way. We've heard from individuals from around the country who have successfully implemented these ongoing goals; they've chosen one personal,*

*one business related, and one dedicated to
serving others. For example:*

Personal Goal: Make sure I get in an early-
morning workout.
*Your personal goal should be something
that will make you feel good. It should inspire,
energize, and motivate you to move forward in
your day with confidence and drive.*

Business Goal: Make ten calls to *new*
business prospects.
*Your professional goal is focused on
improving and building your business. This
example of reaching out to ten new contacts or
prospective clients each day, in addition to
following up and supporting current clients and
completing your regular work-related duties,
shows very specifically how this individual
intends to grow his business.*

Service Goal: Connect two colleagues or
friends who could benefit from the introduction.
*The service goal is never motivated by a sense
of selfishness. It is one you want to attain without
personal or professional gain in mind for yourself
at any level.*

Explore what fires you up and ignites your passion, so
you can routinely create your *Prizefighter Day.* Take your
time. Create three focal points that are activity driven, and that

will give you the sense of accomplishment necessary to create a balanced life personally and professionally.

Before you know it, you will imperceptibly begin to pull away from old disempowering conversations, noting that even an ordinary day is a *Prizefighter Day* on your individual path to greatness.

Prizefighter Day

1.

2.

3.

What can I do to improve tomorrow, based on my performance today?

Living Legacy Exercise

Identify your top five philosophers and philosophies that have impacted your life and will have an impact on your legacy. Each of us is writing the story of his or her own life. At some point in time we will pass our pen to the next generation with lessons to guide them to leave their own legacies.

1.

2.

3.

4.

5.

Go Do Great Things

About the Author

Ben Newman is the founder of *The Continued Fight* and *The Ben Newman Companies*. A four-time author, he also ranks in the top 1 percent of wealth management professionals in the world.

Ben's renowned boot camps, videos, books, blogs, and speaking events empower and inspire thousands of individuals each year to maximize results in their lives, both personally and professionally. Ben has a unique ability to connect with individuals, uncovering the path to their legacy to make a greater difference in the world.

Ben's mother, Janet Fishman Newman, died 11 days before his eighth birthday, leaving a cavernous hole in his universe. Yet while his mother passed away all those years ago, not a single day goes by without the reminder that she helped Ben become the man that he is today. Her strength, love, work ethic, and legacy live on through him, in the family he has created, and the work he does.

He has come to realize she was demonstrating a very important truth—our circumstances in life are much less significant than our responses to them. Ben empowers audiences to embrace adversity in order to achieve success on their path to greatness. His clients have included MARS

Snackfoods, AFA Singapore, The Minnesota Vikings, Northwestern Mutual, New York Life, Mass Financial Group, Boston Medical Center, Australian Gold, Boys & Girls Clubs of America, as well as the thousands of executives, entrepreneurs, and sales teams from around the globe who attend his speeches and seminars.

As the "High Performance Sales Expert," his authentic, powerful, and engaging presentations have become nationally recognized. Ben has shared the stage with Tony Dungy, Colin Powell, Jon Gordon, Dr. Jason Selk, Floyd Little, Aeneas Williams, Walt Jocketty, D'Marco Farr, John O'Leary, Tom Hegna, and other leaders and legends in the field.

Ben lives in his hometown of St. Louis, Missouri, with the true measure of his success, his wife, Ami, and their son, J. Isaac, and daughter, Kennedy Rose.

About the Author

THE BEN NEWMAN COMPANIES

Transforming Obstacles into YOUR Maximum Performance!

Ben Newman speaks to conventions and organizations all over the world. The Ben Newman Companies, a professional speaking and consulting company, conducts boot camps, seminars, and in-depth training in the areas of high performance sales, teamwork, leadership, and relationship building.

Ben's customized speaking and coaching leaves audiences inspired, educated, AND empowered! Participants are able to uncover their true potential, readying them to create the life they are meant to fight for and enjoy. Emerging poised to take on THEIR relentless pursuit of greatness: Their *Prizefighter* day!

If you are interested in purpose-driven programs, based upon the principles of *Own YOUR Success*, contact The Ben Newman Companies.

info@BenNewman.net

★ WWW.BENNEWMAN.NET ★

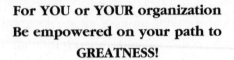

★ www.BenNewman.net ★

For YOU or YOUR organization
Be empowered on your path to
GREATNESS!

- Order Books
- Watch Inspirational Videos
- Order the *Gotta Fight the Shadow of Doubt* DVD
- Attend a Boot Camp, Symposium, or
  Leadership Summit
- Register for *The Continued Fight* Monthly
  Tele-seminar Series
- Sign up for the Free Monthly Newsletter